D0356708

HOW
CAN I GET
THEM TO
LISTEN?

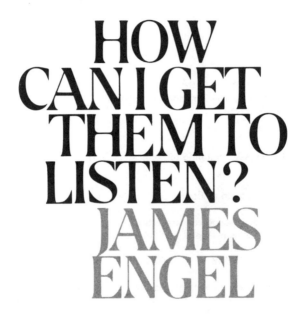

HOW CAN I GET THEM TO LISTEN?

JAMES ENGEL

ZONDERVAN
PUBLISHING HOUSE

OF THE ZONDERVAN CORPORATION | GRAND RAPIDS, MICHIGAN 49506

How Can I Get Them to Listen?
Copyright © 1977 by The Zondervan Corporation
Grand Rapids, Michigan

CIP data

Library of Congress Cataloging in Publication Data

Engel, James F
    How can I get them to listen?

    (Contemporary evangelical perspectives)
    1. Communication—Moral and religious aspects.   2. Communications
research.   I. Title.
P94.E5   808.5'02'42   77-9032

ISBN 0-310-24171-5

Appreciation is expressed to the following for permission to quote
from their Bible translation or paraphrase:

THE LOCKMAN FOUNDATION for the use of the *New American
Standard Bible.* Copyright © 1960, 1962, 1963, 1968, 1971, 1972
by The Lockman Foundation.

TYNDALE HOUSE PUBLISHERS for the use of *The Living Bible.*
Copyright © 1971 by Tyndale House Publishers.

Printed in the United States of America

IN DEDICATION TO
Janet, Joanne, and Susan —
the source of my greatest joy

Contents

Preface

It was in 1972 that God led me to join the staff of the Wheaton Graduate School after a long career in secular marketing research and promotion. I had been a Christian for about seven years and had spent many of these years in evangelism and discipleship of faculty members on the college campus while retaining my position at Ohio State University.

The year 1972 marked the beginning of a new career which basically has been one of blending the principles and procedures of research and strategy into the communication of the Christian message. The years since that time have been a remarkable learning experience, especially as I have had opportunity to conduct training seminars for Christian nationals and missionaries in all parts of the world. My colleagues and I are deeply immersed in the process of discovering what it means to develop a research-based, Spirit-led communication strategy.

These experiences provided the basis for the book coauthored by my friend and dean, Wil Norton, entitled *What's Gone Wrong With the Harvest?*[1] Apparently God has used this small volume both to encourage and to motivate many of His people to adopt a more analytical approach to their ministry. Many now are asking the question, How do I get started in the audience analysis and effectiveness measurements you are advocating? This handbook was written to help the Christian leader develop and implement relatively noncomplicated research projects and to interpret and use the research done by others.

---

[1]This companion volume to this handbook was published in 1975 by the Zondervan Corporation.

I have hesitated to write this book until now, partly because I have been uncertain of the applicability of research principles to the environments of the developing countries. It has been necessary first to build a backlog of experience in Christian research and strategy development. The completion of more than eighty projects at the Wheaton Graduate School has provided a solid basis for my research, although we still have much to learn.

This book was written as a research primer. Many of the complicated issues are avoided. This does not lessen its usefulness, however, because most of the research approaches needed do not demand great methodological sophistication. Enough is said here to enable the reader to get started, and research expertise comes only through experience.

I have written this book especially for my brethren in the developing countries — those national Christian leaders who are hungering for training. Their single-minded desire is to do God's work with maximum effectiveness. It is my prayer that they, as well as colleagues in North America, will be helped in this endeavor through the use of this book.

My greatest debt is to the students in communications at the Wheaton Graduate School. Each has been responsible for initiating, developing, and implementing a field research project in the context of a church or parachurch organization. They are the ones who have spent the most time in the "research trenches" and have provided much of the insight and experience which has enabled this book to be written. I will always be grateful to these friends for what they have taught me over the years as I have worked with them.

Finally, I am appreciative of colleagues in Christian communications research who have contributed their insights to this book. In particular I would like to acknowledge Dr. Ted Haney of the Far Eastern Broadcasting Company, Dr. Donald Miller of the Medical Assistance Program (MAP), and Dr. Donald K. Smith who is Director of Daystar Communications, Inc. in Nairobi, Kenya. Dr. Miller and Dr. Smith also are adjunct members of the Wheaton Communications Faculty. My close friend and colleague at the Graduate School, Richard Senzig, has colabored with me more than anyone else over the past few years. His professional contribution and abiding friendship really have made this book possible. All responsibility for any errors or misstatements, of course, belongs totally to me.

JAMES F. ENGEL
Wheaton, Illinois

1

What Research Is All About

Research is a term fraught with a variety of meanings for the Christian leader. To some it connotes a kind of panacea — a way out of their current dilemmas. Others envisage a panoply of numbers, computers, and statistics, and hence avoid the thought of a return to the horrors of high school algebra. Still others will erect a defense mechanism out of fear that research will point to needed change which, of course, it usually does. Finally, there is a well-meaning group who will object that research and strategy development is unnecessary for the Christian who is relying on the leadership of the Holy Spirit.

Fortunately, research in its essence is a nonthreatening commonplace phenomenon engaged in daily by all of us — the gathering of information for use in decision making. A glance out the window to see if I need to carry an umbrella today is research. A telephone call to see if my neighbor is home before I borrow his lawn mower is research. Most of our fears and misunderstandings will evaporate if we keep our focus on this commonsense role.

It is the purpose of this chapter to discuss why research is necessary in the Christian communication process. The objective is to provide a number of examples and to build a biblical perspective.

A COMMUNICATION CRISIS

"Let the Earth Hear His Voice!" This was the united heart

13

cry of the more than 2,000 who attended the International Congress on World Evangelization at Lausanne and who signed the covenant which reaffirmed their commitment to this cause. But the emotion of this Congress has long since passed. Will such rallying cries as "The Great Commission in This Generation" merely degenerate into platitudes?

Before arriving at an answer, consider these examples:

A church of 650 members seems to be successful from all external measures. But a survey of the congregation revealed that only 20 percent attempted to share their faith in the past month; 30 percent read their Bible as often as three times a week; 21 percent had family devotions; 70 percent confined their church involvement to Sunday services; 10 percent knew their spiritual gift; and 50 percent claimed they are not being fed spiritually in this church.[1]

A Christian-owned radio station offers both secular and Christian programming. It was discovered that programs designed to evangelize the non-Christian are listened to almost entirely by Christians.[2]

Bibles were given to every inmate in a large United States prison. A few days later it was discovered that 90 percent of these found their way into the trash cans, thus causing the unnecessary expenditure of more than $250,000 when this program was prematurely spread to other prisons.

Fewer than 8 percent of the Christians in the seven largest cities of Brazil ever bother to tune in to the many hours of teaching programs directed at them weekly by two major shortwave missionary broadcasters.[3]

---

[1] This church served as the basic example in James F. Engel and H. Wilbert Norton, *What's Gone Wrong With the Harvest?* (Grand Rapids: Zondervan Corporation, 1975).

[2] "A Survey of the K-C-A-M Listening Audience," Central Alaskan Mission (Wheaton Communications Research Report #8, December, 1972).

[3] "The Brazilian Evangelical," Bethany Fellowship (Wheaton Communications Research Report #41, April, 1975).

The plan of salvation was prominently displayed in a magazine directed toward non-Christians on the college campus. It was largely ignored, whereas several articles focusing on a Christian perspective on pertinent issues were both read and positively evaluated.[4]

This list of examples could be extended for many more pages. Notice the common denominator in each: *a reliance on one-way communication.* Messages are *sent* from the pulpit, door-to-door, over the airwaves, or in print. But what is the response? Real communication does not occur until the message is both comprehended and acted upon by the recipient as intended. Communication, in reality, is a two-way process. All too often we ignore the audience.

Can the Word Return Void?

Isaiah 55:11 often is cited as the proof text of one-way Christian communication. God said, " . . . My word . . . shall not return to Me empty [void], without accomplishing what I desire" (NASB). One Christian broadcaster even went so far as to state that he had no responsibility whatsoever other than to air his program and to leave the results to God. When queried on the results he replied, "I haven't the faintest idea — that's God's concern, not mine."

This is not the meaning of the Isaiah passage. It makes reference to the great promises God has given Israel, especially those to be fulfilled after the return of the Messiah. It asserts that God stands behind His covenants, and the purpose was to give comfort. While it is true from other passages in Scripture that spiritual response comes through the ministry of the Holy Spirit, the doctrine of stewardship also underscores the responsibility of the communicator. This responsibility entails, among other things, the necessity to attract the attention of the hearer and to convey the intended message in such a way as to make the Word of God truly relevant.

[4]"Collegiate Challenge Readership," Campus Crusade for Christ (Wheaton Communications Research Report #11, April, 1973).

The "leave-it-to-God" attitude is all too common, and it reflects both poor biblical exegesis and faulty stewardship.

People Are Not Robots

We cannot ignore the fact that the recipient of the message has a God-given ability to see and hear what he or she wants to see and hear. The message must pass through a filter containing learned patterns of thinking, behaving, attitudes, and personality traits. Thousands of published and unpublished studies demonstrate conclusively that unwanted messages can be avoided entirely *(selective attention),* miscomprehended *(selective distortion),* or forgotten *(selective retention).*[5] Christian communication is not exempt from this filtering process as Jess Moody clearly states:

> The church needs to be informed that the world isn't obligated to pay any attention to us. I am convinced that they will when we deserve to be heard. We must merit an audience.[6]

Communication Begins With the Audience

Many years ago, I spent a period of time with a major advertising agency. A team of writers and artists had laboriously prepared a series of ads for a fabric softener. The chief executive on this account made an interesting comment after viewing these efforts: "These are very creative, but. . . . " His "but," of course, was the question "Will they sell the product?"

Too many of us in Christian work are like this advertising team — we are message centered. We know what we think the audience should hear and do our best to get it to them, often sparing no expense in the form of the best printing presses, powerful transmitters, dramatic pulpit mannerisms, and so on. But what good is all this effort if it is not speaking in relevant terms, helping people to struggle with the real issues of their

---

[5]This evidence is reviewed in Engel and Norton, *What's Gone Wrong?* ch. 2. Also see James F. Engel, David T. Kollat, and Roger D. Blackwell, *Consumer Behavior,* rev. ed. (Hinsdale, Ill.: Dryden Press, 1973), ch. 8.

[6]Jess Moody, "A Drink at Joel's Place," *Today* (August 24, 1969), p. 3.

lives? All the creative finesse and media muscle in the world will go for naught if we are not speaking to the audience where they are. This principle, in itself, is the strongest single argument for the use of research. People cannot be understood if the communicator remains in his or her armchair safely protected from the world out there.

Removing the Cobwebs of Misunderstanding

Returning to the question which opened this section, yes, there is a real danger that world evangelization will only be a slogan or even a myth. The great need now is to replace what Ted Ward calls our "Fuzzy Fables of Communications"[7] with research-based strategies which are appropriate for a modern and changing world. Surprisingly enough, the key lies far less in the use of modern technology than in a return to a truly biblical perspective on Spirit-led planning.

A BIBLICAL PERSPECTIVE ON RESEARCH AND PLANNING

Not long ago I heard a well-known business executive proclaim that any Christian organization will succeed only if it applies modern management principles. While this is only a partial truth, most management experts would agree that planning should progress through the following stages (Figure 1).

1. Analysis of the environment
2. Establishment of measurable goals
3. Determination of communication strategy
4. Execution of communication strategy
5. Analysis of effectiveness
6. Evaluation (post mortem)

Figure 1. A Model of Strategic Planning

---

[7]Ted Ward, "Fuzzy Fables of Communications That Count," *Christian Communications Spectrum,* vol. 1 (Winter, 1975), pp. 10,11.

The error enters in assuming that this process belongs exclusively to the province of secular management because its roots lie in the Book of Proverbs. King Solomon observed that "Any enterprise is built by wise planning, becomes strong through common sense, and profits wonderfully by keeping abreast of the facts" (Prov. 24:3,4, *Living Bible*). He pointed out (also from the *Living Bible*) that analysis of the environment is the logical first step: "It is dangerous and sinful to rush into the unknown (19:2); "A sensible man watches for problems ahead and prepares to meet them" (27:12). The Christian *is* to make plans: "We should make plans — *counting on God to direct us*" (16:9) (italics mine). The distinction in Christian work, of course, is unwavering reliance on the direction of the Spirit of God.

Also, we are commanded to measure effectiveness and to change plans where necessary: "Anyone willing to be corrected is on the pathway to life" (10:17); "A man who refuses to admit his mistakes can never be successful" (28:13). The ever-present danger is that "A man may ruin his chances by his own foolishness and then blame it on the Lord" (19:3).

A logical, disciplined approach to planning, therefore, is not an option for the Christian, because in this process we are cooperating with God as He leads through His Spirit. Prayer thus becomes a continual necessity, not a mere appendix which says, in effect, "Lord, please bless what we have already decided to do." John R. W. Stott has put it well:

> Some say rather piously that the Holy Spirit is himself the complete and satisfactory solution to the problem of communication, and indeed that when he is present and active, then communication ceases to be a problem. What on earth does such a statement mean? Do we now have liberty to be as obscure, confused and irrelevant as we like, and the Holy Spirit will make all things plain? To use the Holy Spirit to rationalize our laziness is nearer blasphemy than piety. Of course *without* the Holy Spirit all our explanations are futile. But this is not to say that *with* the Holy Spirit they are also futile. For the Holy Spirit chooses to work through them. Trust in the Holy Spirit must not

be used as a device to save us the labour of biblical and contemporary studies.[8]

Research and the Planning Process

Any decision maker must approach a problem initially with two assets: (1) intuition and analytical ability and (2) experience. These are becoming increasing incomplete in our rapidly changing world. The missing ingredient is research. Visualize a three-legged stool with only two legs in place. Obviously it cannot stand. Add the third leg and it will function beautifully. Research is this third leg which must be restored to its proper place.

How does research fit into the planning process. Figure 2 should be studied frequently because it will be referred to often throughout the book. Notice that research enters stages 1, 3, and 5 in the planning process.

PLANNING STAGE	RESEARCH INPUT
1. Analysis of the environment	Environmental description (assessment of audience spiritual status, competition, and other factors which define the opportunities and limitations for strategy)
2. Establishment of measurable goals	
3. Determination of communication strategy	Pretesting the response to alternate plans
4. Execution of communication strategy	
5. Analysis of effectiveness	Assessment of message comprehension, retention, and response
6. Evaluation (post-mortem)	

Figure 2. The Role of Research in Spirit-led Planning

[8]John R. W. Stott, *Christian Mission in the World* (Downers Grove, Ill.: InterVarsity Press, 1976), p. 127. Reprinted with special permission.

Environmental Description. Jesus left a remarkable example during His life on earth. His was not a "canned message" replete with spiritual cliches. Rather, He built a bond of trust by using the vernacular and speaking to the needs of people. His message varied continuously, depending upon the situation He faced. How did He know so much about His audience? He met people on the streets, on the hillsides, in the fields, at work, at prayer, on the roads, at weddings, at meals. In short, He used observational research which then was energized by the Holy Spirit to bring about remarkable results. Moreover, He could legitimately say that we will do even greater things if we rely upon the same Holy Spirit.

Jesus keenly recognized differences between people — some were open and receptive and others were not. He rebuked the Pharisees by His cutting comment that "I have not come to call righteous men but sinners to repentance" (Luke 5:32, NASB). He said, in effect, "Go your way with your closed filters, and I will concentrate on those who feel a need for what I have to say." In so doing, He established a fundamental principle of communications strategy: *concentrate primarily on receptive audience segments.* Notice that this does not call for abandonment of the nonreceptive but rather for a focus on those from whom the harvest will be the greatest.

The apostle Paul also left a useful example. His primary approach to people was to " . . . try to find a common ground with him so that he will let me tell him about Christ and let Christ save him" (1 Cor. 9:22, *Living Bible).* People respond when the communicator undertakes the analysis required to discover felt needs and the proper ways to convey biblical truth so that it truly is "sharper than a two-edged sword."

Placing this approach in contemporary perspective, the Greater Vancouver Canada Reachout with Leighton Ford was initiated by a survey of the spiritual awareness and felt needs of high school youth and adults. Among the adults, it was found that 61 percent consistently claimed to be completely satisfied with life as it was and felt no need for any changes.[9] Religion was seen largely as irrelevant to the majority. The Vancouver analysis uncovered some segments, however, which gave different responses. Among these the most promising target for Christian communication proved to be the man or woman over thirty making more than $20,000 a year as a family. The husband, in particular, voiced concern that his job no longer offered the satisfaction it once did. Both spouses stated a fear that children may stray because of their inability as parents to bridge the generation gap. In addition, others commented that their marriages were eroding. Few of these people were actively involved in religion, but they showed considerable interest in exploring the truths of Christianity. So here we have a promising segment — evidencing felt need for change and a definite pattern of needs to which the power of the gospel may be related. Without this type of research, this promising audience target easily could have been missed and a potential harvest gone unreaped.

Pretesting of Strategy. Once a program is prepared to meet the opportunities disclosed by the environmental analysis, there is much to be gained by pretesting the strategy prior to investment of large amounts of funds. Consider the following examples:

> Out of a group of some fifty radio spot announcements aimed at stimulating Bible reading among listeners to American Forces Radio, no more than eight were found to be acceptable for a more general audience. There was little evidence that *any* of these eight, in turn, would achieve their stated purpose of encouraging Bible reading among non-Christians.[10]

> Out of more than 100 American Christian films tested in an African country, only a handful were correctly comprehended by the audience and hence proved to be suitable for showing.

---

[9] "Spiritual Status Analysis, Vancouver Adults," Leighton Ford Evangelistic Association (Wheaton Communications Research Report #56, December, 1975).

[10] "An Analysis of Project Linklines" (Wheaton Communications Research Report #29, July, 1974).

It appeared that high school youth in Quito, Ecuador could be reached through use of photo novels (foto novellas) written with a Christian slant. Pretests of such a photo novel, however, disclosed that most would not read this type of book and would respond much more quickly to radio. A Christian-oriented rock radio program was substituted as a more appropriate strategy.[11]

Bibles have been distributed to telephone owners in some parts of the world with at least a modest degree of success. A pretest of this strategy in one Asian country indicated that most would discard the Bibles if this method were utilized in that situation. Obviously a different strategy was undertaken.

It is obvious that the time taken to pretest in each of the above situations was highly productive in that faulty strategy was discovered prior to the investment of extensive amounts of money and manpower. Increasingly the pretest will be an indispensible part of the arsenal of the Christian communicator just as it has been in the secular world since the 1940s.

Measurement of Effectiveness. Christian stewardship calls for analysis of effectiveness, assuming that measurable goals have been set (Figure 2). Only then is it possible to learn from successes and failures. Fortunately, increasing numbers of Christian organizations are sensing the need to undertake this step, and the gains can be great as these examples illustrate:

A large group of Japanese pastors and laymen were trained in one approach to personal evangelism, sent out to witness, and returned with reports of hundreds who allegedly received Christ. A followup analysis disclosed, however, that the "prayer of commitment" usually did not result in conversion and was, instead, mostly a response of courtesy. It was obvious that changes were needed in an American designed evangelistic strategy.

A large mission board surveyed its supporting clientele and

---

[11]"Algo Nuevo: HCJB" (Wheaton Communications Research Report #58, December, 1975).

discovered that many gave totally wrong answers when queried on basic details about the nature of the mission, its fields of service, and the varieties of ministry. This led to a revamping of communications directed to both the financial contributor and the noncontributor.

It has traditionally been assumed that Brazilians will respond to translations of American books. The largest potential market, however, was found to be in the Assembly of God church, composed mostly of members of lower socioeconomic classes. Some Christian leaders assumed such people are not readers. Research disclosed that they are reading photo novels and comic books, but not the translated American books. Plans now are under way to write a whole new series of Christian books in this format to speak to a variety of felt needs within the church membership.[12]

TO SUM UP

Research, along with intuition and experience, is an indispensable aspect of the arsenal of the Christian communicator. It is a necessity in a rapidly changing world because there is no other accurate way to find the pulse of the audience. There also is a strong biblical mandate to provide solid information for use in planning. Research does not short-circuit the work of the Holy Spirit but rather provides an essential avenue through which He can lead. The objective is to avoid the dilemma stated in this paraphrase of a little doggerel by Kenneth Boulding:

> Christian communication is like a blunderbuss.
> For all our muss and fuss,
> We fire a monstrous charge of shot,
> And sometimes hit but mostly not.

Environmental description, pretesting, and measurements of effectiveness can be of major value in substituting a rifle shot for the blunderbuss.

It is the purpose of this book to equip the reader to carry out

[12]James F. Engel, "An End to Guesswork in Christian Book Publishing," *Christian Communications Spectrum,* vol. 1 (Fall-Winter, 1975), p. 19.

some of the basic types of research which have been outlined here. No one can become an expert just by reading a brief manual, but this is a starting point. A second objective is to place this important subject in a distinctly crosscultural framework so that the manual will be of use to those working in a variety of circumstances. Obviously it will be impossible in a few pages to describe all the variations which will be necessary, but hopefully enough can be said to permit successful adaptation of research methodology in most settings.

For Further Reading

Churchill, Gilbert A., Jr. *Marketing Research*. Hinsdale, Ill.: The Dryden Press, 1976.

Engel, James F. and Norton, H. Wilbert. *What's Gone Wrong With the Harvest?* Grand Rapids, Mich.: Zondervan Corporation, 1975.

Kelley, Eugene J. *Marketing Planning and Competitive Strategy*. Englewood Cliffs, N.J.: Prentice-Hall, Inc., 1972.

Mass Media Research Workshop (held in the Netherlands, 1973). Geneva, Switzerland: Lutheran World Federation: Department of Studies, 1974.

Stott, John R. W. *Christian Mission in the World*. Downers Grove, Ill.: InterVarsity Press, 1976.

Zaltman, Gerald and Burger, Philip C. *Marketing Research Fundamentals and Dynamics*. Hinsdale, Ill.: The Dryden Press, 1975.

2

Thinking the Problem Through

It is not surprising that research is a process which has many steps. These phases are outlined in Figure 3, which should be studied carefully. It provides the structure for the remainder of this manual.

1. Definition of the problem

2. Identification of data requirements
   a. Categories of data needed to solve the problem
   b. Sources of the data needed to solve the problem

3. Determination of the data collection procedure
   a. Observation
   b. Descriptive survey
   c. Experimental design

4. Design of the sampling plan

5. Construction of the data collection instrument

6. Data collection in the field

7. Tabulation, analysis, and reporting of data

8. Phasing research into strategy

Figure 3. The Stages in the Research Process

This chapter focuses on the first two phases which almost always prove to be most crucial for the success of the entire project: (1) definition of the problem and (2) identification of data requirements. If the problem is not conceptualized properly, all the skill in the world in research design and execution will go for naught. When all is said and done, research will be of value only when: (1) it is undertaken for the right reasons; (2) it sheds light on real problems; and (3) it actually is phased into strategy.

PROBLEM DEFINITION

It is commonly felt among marketing researchers that 50 percent or more of the research undertaken in the business world winds up collecting dust on a shelf somewhere without having made the slightest impact on decision. Such a waste of scarce resources is bad enough in any setting, but it is even more indefensible from the perspective of Christian stewardship. Therefore, it is essential from the beginning to specify (1) *why the research is being done;* (2) *the nature of the real problem;* and (3) *what will be done with the data once it is collected.*

Why Is the Research Being Done?

Some Improper Motivations

(1) Everyone else is doing it. It has been interesting to watch the progression of fads in Christian circles. The training program of one mission board has focused in recent years first on church growth theory, then on principles of management, and now on communication strategy and research. One veteran was heard to say "What do you suppose will be the hot topic next year?"

Communication research has not yet become so widespread that it can be labeled as a fad, but there is the danger that the groundswell which is building will degenerate into a type of bandwagon on which everyone feels compelled to jump, regardless of the need. The result easily could be unneeded research. In the final analysis the undertaking of research should never be motivated by what another person does.

(2) A search for the "holy grail." A research team had just finished giving a report which verified that a Christian publisher was pursuing the right course in his current strategy. The first response was, "What a disappointment; I thought we would learn something new!"

Research should not be viewed as a magic key which opens doors that previously have been undiscovered by experience and intuition. This often happens, of course, but it is equally common to discover that research has largely verified previously established hunches. The benefit from the research is *greater certainty that the right strategy is being pursued.* It should never be overlooked that intuition, experience, and research all work together in determination of strategy.

(3) A mandate from "above." Several years ago, a research project stirred up quite a hornet's nest in a Christian organization. The conclusion was unmistakable: the magazine under analysis was not attracting readers. Soon the organizational grapevine was activated with the message that this research was no good in the first place. It was promptly buried in the files and never acted upon.

Why did this happen? At a much later period it was discovered that the editor was forced by his board to authorize this project. He actively fought it most of the way but kept his objections largely to himself. Whatever his personal reasons, he was determined not to implement the recommendations, particularly after the findings turned out to be uncomplimentary.

There must be a commitment by management *at all levels,* especially at the level of implementation, to take research seriously and to change when it is clear that change is warranted. All this project served to do was to make temporary waves in an otherwise smooth organizational pond. One obviously cannot condone the poor stewardship exhibited here, but it also is true that the project never should have been undertaken initially without full assurance of managerial support.

(4) To convince everyone that "I am right." Sometimes research is undertaken to prove a point. A certain group in a

large church was openly advocating a change in the evening service toward more body life and sharing. On the expectation that others felt the same way, these leaders confidently authorized a survey of the congregation on the assumption that their case would be buttressed. Much to their surprise (and dismay), the results came out quite the opposite. Most of those surveyed wanted the service to remain pretty much as it was. This, of course, is a case of the mind being made up before the facts. Nothing was resolved by all the expenditure of funds and research effort.

Proper Expectations for Research. It has been stressed several times that research does not replace intuition and experience. Rather it serves to augment these essential qualities of a successful manager and to reduce, but not eliminate, the chances for decision error. This, of course, is an enormous contribution in and of itself. Illumination can be provided into previously unlit avenues of inquiry; preliminary insights can be sharpened; hunches can be verified. In a world of rapid change, there often is no substitute for research, but there always will be a remaining element of uncertainty. This uncertainty probably is a good thing, because most of us otherwise would ignore prayer and do it our way.

What Is the Real Problem?

When this chapter was being written in first draft, I was interrupted by a long-distance phone call which contained the following request: "We have just finished a new series of evangelistic tapes. Can you help us determine if they are effective?"

There was no quick answer to this question. The first step was to define exactly what was meant by "effectiveness." It can be measured at several levels in the communication process:

1. How many people actually buy the tapes and listen to them when they are distributed for sale? (exposure)

2. What proportion of the exposed audience grasps the main point? (comprehension)

3. Is the content retained for longer than just a few minutes? (retention)

4. What attitudinal and behavioral changes result? (results)

The last question is especially critical, because it presumes that specific measurable objectives have been previously established. Unfortunately, this rarely proves to be the case.

I once asked the head of a major evangelistic organization what the objectives of his organization were. The answer given was "to lead the maximum number of people to Christ." But what does it actually mean to "lead people to Christ"? Who is the target audience? How will we know once they actually have accepted Christ?

It should be apparent to the reader by now that problem definition usually is the single most difficult step in the entire research process. Fuzzy statements of intent must be sharpened, and this can take hours of give and take before any degree of precision emerges. Unfortunately, vague goals and platitudinous statements of philosophy can sound so Christian while serving, at the same time, as a convenient way to avoid accountability. Some never will take that step toward specificity for this reason.

Assuming a proper attitude of accountability, it generally is possible to arrive at workable problem definitions. One Christian magazine editor began initially with the request that the effectiveness of his magazine be evaluated. Probing questions were directed toward the specific objectives underlying this publishing effort. Initially they were fuzzy, but precision emerged through brainstorming, with the following research questions isolated:

1. What percentage of those who receive this magazine actually read any of the content of a given issue?

2. For the last issue, what proportion recalled reading each of

the articles? Were they only skimmed, or were they read mostly in entirety?

3. Could each person who claimed to have read a given article actually state its main point? (Unfortunately the main point of several articles was obscure at best.)

4. For each of the three lead articles, did the reader evaluate them as useful for his or her life?

5. What are the five most important felt needs that readers would like to see addressed in future issues?

6. What other Christian magazines are being subscribed to or read by thise readers who are being surveyed?

7. What are the background characteristics of respondents (the more technical term here is "demographic characteristics" which usually refers to such factors as age, income, sex, and so on)?

Now it was possible to design a readership study which would result in useful decision-making data.

How Will the Data Be Used?

Phasing research into strategy is the last step in the research process outlined in Figure 3. Yet, it cannot be disregarded at the outset for the reason that unused research is an unwarranted luxury.

A commitment to act upon research findings must never be assumed. Rather, it must be verified at the outset. One key is to ascertain that each item of information really is needed in planning and decision making. This calls for a cost/benefit analysis. The purpose is to verify the actual decision-making benefits of the project against its costs. If the costs are seen to outweigh the gains, changes should be made, or the entire project aborted if necessary.

Cost/benefit analysis should extend to every phase in the research design. The types of projects discussed in this manual usually are not costly, and most are in the range of a few hundred to a few thousand dollars. Nevertheless, significant modifications can always be made to hold down costs. Often one sacrifices an item of data or perhaps a degree of precision in methodology for cost reasons. This type of decision is known as a "tradeoff" in which something is sacrificed to make a gain elsewhere. The concept of tradeoff will receive frequent mention in the comingpages.

IDENTIFICATION OF DATA REQUIREMENTS

Stage 2 of the research process (Figure 3) is to assess both the categories of needed data and the sources from which it can be gathered.

Categories of Data

Christian organizations often must serve two distinct and non-overlapping audiences: (1) the target audiences for evangelistic and/or disciple-building communication and (2) the supportive clientele who pay the bills. Obviously the specifics of each task vary sharply, but there is a common core of data outlined in Figure 4 which must be acquired in order to be successful at each.

1. Awareness: what they know and comprehend about the subject(s) under consideration.

2. Attitudes: how they feel about the subject(s) under consideration.

3. Life styles: important motivations and felt needs which affect the way in which communication is seen as being relevant to the individual.

4. Decision-making styles: the manner in which audience members arrive at decisions with respect to the subject(s) under consideration, including the effects of interaction with family members and other significant individuals as well as patterns of media exposure.

**Figure 4. Audience Information Needed to
Determine Communication Strategy**

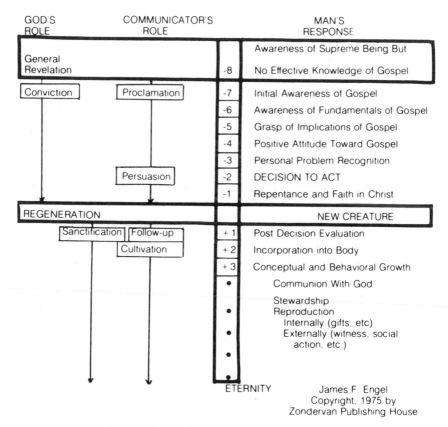

GOD'S ROLE	COMMUNICATOR'S ROLE		MAN'S RESPONSE
General Revelation		-8	Awareness of Supreme Being But No Effective Knowledge of Gospel
Conviction	Proclamation	-7	Initial Awareness of Gospel
		-6	Awareness of Fundamentals of Gospel
		-5	Grasp of Implications of Gospel
		-4	Positive Attitude Toward Gospel
		-3	Personal Problem Recognition
	Persuasion	-2	DECISION TO ACT
		-1	Repentance and Faith in Christ
REGENERATION			NEW CREATURE
Sanctification	Follow-up	+1	Post Decision Evaluation
	Cultivation	+2	Incorporation into Body
		+3	Conceptual and Behavioral Growth
		•	Communion With God
		•	Stewardship Reproduction Internally (gifts, etc) Externally (witness, social action, etc.)
		•	
		•	

ETERNITY

James F. Engel
Copyright, 1975 by
Zondervan Publishing House

Figure 5 The Spiritual Decision Process

Understanding the Audience for Evangelism and Discipleship. This, of course, is intended as a companion volume to *What's Gone Wrong With the Harvest?* and many are familiar with the audience-decision model which underlies its whole approach.[1] Nevertheless, it is helpful to review it briefly because it contains the keys to understanding the type of data required in design of an effective Christian communication strategy. This model is reproduced in Figure 5.

Everyone falls somewhere on this continuum in terms of his or her relationship to Christ. Some may lie at the first stage (-8) in which they have only a dim grasp of the essence of God through nature, conscience, or some other forms of general revelation. Others understand more fully the fundamental truths of the gospel, especially the truths of monotheism, the sinful nature of man, and the uniqueness of Jesus. Accordingly, they will fall somewhere in between positions -7 and -3, depending upon the level of both awareness and comprehension as well as positive attitude toward the knowledge they possess. God has begun the ministry of conviction, and the role for the Christian communicator is one of proclamation — building essential awareness and bringing about a response of interest and attitude change.

People at stages -8 through -4 have not, as yet, reached the point where there is strong-felt need for change and the accompanying motivation to open themselves to serious consideration of a commitment to Jesus Christ. This can occur only where there is a grasp of the implications of the gospel, accompanied by positive attitude and personal problem recognition (stage -3, at which point the individual perceives an intolerable gap between *what is* and *what might be*). The person now is open to a challenge for decision, referred to here as a ministry of persuasion. The only options are to reject the message or to repent and commit the life to Christ by faith, thus becoming a new creation (a sovereign ministry of God through regeneration). In the event of rejection, the communicator must drop

---

[1]Engel and Norton, *What's Gone Wrong?* p. 44.

back to stress once again the implications of the message to make certain they were fully grasped.

The Christian growth process begins after the new birth. The first stage (+ 1) often is one of post-decision evaluation accompanied by doubts and anxiety concerning the validity and permanence of the decision. God's role now is to initiate the process of sanctification, and the communicator has the responsibility of follow-up. It is necessary once again to stress the basic truths of the gospel and the meaning of faith. Simultaneously the new believer is assimilated into the fellowship of the body of Christ, usually through the formal means of baptism (+ 2). Now spiritual growth begins in earnest through the ministry of cultivation, and it occurs in three dimensions: (1) communion with God through prayer and worship; (2) stewardship of resources; and (3) reproduction internally within the body of Christ and externally through various forms of witness. Growth, in turn, continues until one actually goes to be with Christ.

The objective of Christian communication is to move people from one stage to another, as communicator and Holy Spirit work together in their respective ministries. The four ministries of proclamation, persuasion, follow-up, and cultivation all are qualitatively different and are essential aspects of the total work of the church.

Any of these communication ministries will, at best, be a hit and miss affair without the following specific information:

1. Biblical awareness —
   a. For the nonbeliever (stages -8 through -1): awareness and grasp of the truths about the nature of God, the nature of man as a sinner, and the claims of Jesus Christ.
   b. For the believer (stages + 1 through eternity): awareness and grasp of the essential doctrines of the faith.

2. Attitudes. Both the believer and the nonbeliever possess evaluative responses toward the church and the Christian message. If negative, these can be potent inhibitors to desired progression in the decision process. Attitude change thus often is an important communication goal.

3. Life styles. It is a demonstrated communication principle that people respond when a message on any subject is shown to be relevant in terms of their basic motivations and felt needs. Thus it is necessary to focus an inquiry on those aspects of general life style and felt needs which are relevant at the moment.

4. Decision-making styles. Everyone comes to Christ and grows in the faith through different means. Some are greatly influenced by other people, especially members of the immediate family. Others are profoundly affected by the mass media. The question here centers on the sources of information and the importance of each in stimulating change in the decision process.

This, of course, is only a brief outline. Other chapters will examine each category of information in much greater depth. For now, however, this is a sufficient guideline in development of the initial project phases.

Understanding the Supportive Clientele. Not every Christian communicator must rely on a clientele for both financial and prayer support, but nearly everyone is accountable to some parent body. The cultivation of such individuals thus can assume considerable importance.

As of this writing almost twenty organizations have asked the communications staff and faculty at the Wheaton Graduate School to evaluate clientele response to their programs and communication methods. These inquiries usually follow the outline in Figure 4 quite closely, although there are obvious variations from one study to the next. For example, it often is necessary to investigate readership of magazines and other forms of promotional materials. Awareness and attitude, however, are essential information. In addition, the organization must assess the motivations of clientele if they are to relate to both donors and nondonors in truly relevant fashion.

Sources of Information

Most of the discussion here has focused on surveys which are tailor-made for a given audience. But one should never undertake a survey if information is available elsewhere. Reference thus should be made at the outset to both published and unpublished secondary sources. Many countries have valuable census information which can give considerable insight into audience characteristics. Other governmental agencies such as UNESCO frequently publish reports which contain much valuable data. The anthropological literature, in addition, may give enough background about a given group of people to make a survey unnecessary. The library therefore is the starting point. Surveys are undertaken only when available information is found to be incomplete.

To Sum Up

This chapter has provided an overview of the research process and has focused, in particular, on the first two stages: (1) problem definition and (2) identification of categories and sources of needed information. Problem definition was shown to encompass some perplexing discussions centering on the motivation for the project and the relevance of the information for decision making. Indeed, this is the single most demanding stage of the entire process. It cannot be stressed too frequently that everything else is a total waste unless a proper foundation has been built from the outset.

It was suggested that the categories of audience information, in general, fall into four categories: (1) awareness; (2) attitude; (3) life style; and (4) decision-making style. The specific information, of course, will vary depending upon the audience focus. Is the intent to evangelize the nonbeliever and/or to build the believer in the faith? Or is the purpose to build the loyalty and support of clientele? The author's model of the spiritual decision-making process was reviewed to provide insight into the first of these two essential tasks and the information which is required for effective strategy.

For Further Reading

Backstrom, Charles H. and Hursh, Gerald D. *Survey Research.* Evanston, Ill.: Northwestern University Press, 1963, ch. 1.

Boyd, Harper W., Jr., and Westfall, Ralph. *Marketing Research: Text and Cases.* Homewood, Ill.: Richard D. Irwin, Inc., 1972, ch. 1.

Bross, Irwin D. J. *Design for Decision.* New York: The Free Press, 1965.

Engel, James F. and Norton, H. Wilbert, *What's Gone Wrong With the Harvest?* Grand Rapids, Mich.: Zondervan Corporation, 1975, chs. 2 and 3.

Schaller, Lyle E. *The Change Agent.* Nashville, Tenn.: Abingdon Press, 1972.

3

The Data Collection Procedure

Having defined the problem and evaluated the data requirements, the next step in the research process outlined in Figure 3 is to determine the data collection procedure. More specifically, should we use observation, a descriptive survey, or an experimental design? And, if the problem calls for a survey, what type of survey should it be — telephone, personal interview, direct mail, or some combination of all three?

Before looking at these issues in more detail, it is necessary to define three important terms which will receive frequent usage from here on, at which time the implications will emerge in sharper focus:

Error: the extent to which data collected from a subset of a larger population fails to reflect the actual information which would emerge if this larger population were surveyed in entirety. In other words, this is a measure of the inaccuracy which can result from using a sample.

Bias: inaccuracy in survey data resulting from faulty steps in the research design process itself other than sampling. Examples would be misleading questioning procedures and data interpretation contaminated by a desire to prove a point.

Research cost: obviously this refers to the outlays necessitated to collect and analyze data using a particular type of research design.

How Can I Get Them to Listen?

Each type of collection procedure to be reviewed in the following pages offers its own unique combination of error, bias, and cost. The objective always is to reduce error and bias levels to the lowest possible degree consistent with cost constraints.

THE RESEARCH DESIGN

There are three general categories of research design: (1) *observation;* (2) *descriptive survey;* and (3) *experiment.*

Observation.

A Christian publisher was interested in which of two possible cover designs would be most effective in stimulating sales of a new Bible translation. One obviously could ask people which they liked best, but this may not reflect their actual choice in a real life situation. A better procedure would be to observe which option actually is chosen when the two versions are offered for sale side by side.

Observation is one of the most inexpensive forms of research, and there are a number of occasions when it is the only valid approach. One obvious advantage is that it is "unobtrusive"[1] — i.e., there is no need to have someone ask questions and thereby incur the potential bias from this source. It is a favorite tool of the anthropologist who frequently can learn as much from systematic observation as anyone ever could from broad-scale surveying.[2]

The disadvantages are equally obvious. First, the observer never can be totally free from interpretation bias. Everything must be processed through his or her own filter of values, information, and attitudes. Also, many items of needed information simply cannot be observed. How, for example, could

---

[1]Eugene J. Webb, Donald T. Campbell, Richard D. Schwartz, and Lee Sechrest, *Unobtrusive Measures: Nonreactive Research in the Social Sciences* (Chicago: Rand McNally & Company, 1966).

[2]See, for example, Frank W. Moore (ed.), *Readings in Cross-Cultural Methodology* (New Haven, Conn.: Human Relations Area Files Press, 1961).

one observe the extent of a person's knowledge about the life and claims of Jesus Christ?

The Descriptive Survey

Observation, then, is limited in its scope. Recourse often must be made to some type of first-hand questioning when one's purpose is evangelism or discipleship. If the audience target is one person, then structured conversation will suffice. When the numbers are larger it is necessary to undertake a survey of a representative cross section of the audience in question. This survey, in effect, is equivalent to a snapshot of reality at a given point in time. Therefore, the survey is limited to description, and underlying causal factors must be inferred rather than actually observed in their dynamics.

The use of a sample, of course, immediately introduces sampling error. In addition, bias can enter in questionnaire design, in interviewing, in tabulation, and in analysis. Error and bias can be reduced, however, and this serves as the main underlying purpose of a manual such as this.

The Experiment

Assume that a new program of theological education by extension has been designed for use by church leaders in a given geographic area. Will it be superior to the training methods now in use? A descriptive survey really cannot answer this question. Therefore, it will be necessary to design an experiment in which the researcher "manipulates" or changes some variables (in this case the method of training) while holding all other things constant. This is the essence of an experimental design.[3]

A simple experiment might call for segregation of leaders into three equivalent groups, one of which receives the new material. A second group would be taught using existing

---

[3]The classic reference is Donald T. Campbell and Julian C. Stanley, *Experimental and Quasi-Experimental Designs for Research* (Chicago: Rand Mc-Nally & Company, 1966).

methods, and a third group would receive no training at all. It is referred to as a control group. Various measures of learning then would be utilized for the first two groups and a comparison made at a later point to see which of the teaching methods produces the greatest response. The control group documents what would happen if nothing at all had been done and thus provides a good bench mark against which to assess the actual effects of the training methods.

The experimental design also suffers from a number of measurement biases, but this subject is beyond the scope of this manual.[4] Also it tends to be the most costly and demanding of all research approaches.

Choosing the Appropriate Research Design

Research objectives always are the starting point in the design decision. If they are stated with sufficient precision, the most appropriate design usually will be apparent. At times cost limitations will favor one approach over another, but usually it is possible to modify any of the above methods so that costs can be reduced without undue sacrifice of required data. This is the issue of the "tradeoff" discussed above.

This manual is confined to discussion of the descriptive survey. This is not to say that it always is preferable. Rather, the types of questions most often asked by communicators can best be answered with surveys in many instances.

Types of Surveys

Survey designs fall into three basic categories: (1) *personal interview;* (2) *telephone interviews;* and (3) *direct mail.* For ease of reference, the advantages and disadvantages of each are summarized in Figure 6. In the selection of one over another we always should weigh these criteria: ease of data collection, speed of data collection, ability to achieve wide geographic coverage, quantity of data obtainable, accuracy of data obtainable, and cost.

---

[4]These are outlined clearly in the above source.

CRITERION	PERSONAL INTERVIEW	TELEPHONE INTERVIEW	DIRECT MAIL
Ease of data collection	Highly flexible, permitting use of interviewer probes, complex rating scales. Ability to alter the flow of questioning during the course of the interview.	Somewhat flexible in that the interviewer may alter the flow and probe for clarification. Inflexible to the extent that complex rating scales cannot be administered over the telephone.	Inflexible and commited to a fixed written survey instrument with no opportunity to modify question flow or probe for meaning.
Speed of data collection	Very time consuming because of difficulties in contacting respondents and the time involved in conducting the interview itself.	Quickest of all methods. Data collection is virtually instantaneous if many telephone interviewers are used.	Very time consuming. May prohibit its use. Generally responses come in slowly and require a period of six to eight weeks.
Geographic coverage	Limited by expense of interviewer travel.	Limited only by actual expense of telephone time.	No problem at all, and this is one of the greatest advantages of this method.
Quantity of data obtainable	Generally not a problem, assuming the subject is of interest to the respondent and interviewer establishes a good relationship.	Decidedly limited. Usually interviews cannot exceed 10-15 minutes.	Not a problem. Unduly long questionnaires reduce response rates, but this also is a function of respondent interest in the subject.
Accuracy of data obtainable	Excellent, due to the presence of the interviewer limits ability to probe. Limited by the bias of the interviewer's presence. Some may be reluctant to reveal truth.	Open to question. Generally not a problem if interview is limited to relatively nonthreatening subjects.	Opportunity provided for careful reflection and thoughtful reply. Absence of interviewer limits ability to probe and clarify. Incomplete answers are common.
Cost	Usually most expensive, especially if sample is large and geographic coverage is extensive.	Quite inexpensive if calls are made locally. Long distance rates are a limitation.	If return rates are adequate, this is the least expensive method, all things considered. If returns are low, the cost per respondent may be quite high.

**Figure 6. The Advantages and Disadvantages
of Three Survey Strategies**

How Can I Get Them to Listen?

The Personal Interview

Many would allege that the personal interview is preferable, all things being equal, for the reason that the presence of the interviewer permits greater ability to probe and clarify answers. On the other hand, the presence of an interviewer can be a real source of bias, especially when approaching people in the developing countries. People often are unwilling to bare their innermost thoughts completely to another person, and the presence of the interviewer does not permit anonymity. Moreover, some have a tendency to reply in the manner they feel will most please the interviewer. Valid data cannot be collected under such circumstances.

These problems of bias can be mitigated by skillful research design. A major survey was undertaken among Brazilian Christians, and it was necessary to have an interviewer available.[5] Respondents were only marginally literate at best, and questions had to be explained. Yet, the cultural norm of courtesy raised the real threat that the replies would reveal only "what the interviewer wanted to hear." Recourse was made to a modified group interview. People gathered in groups of ten, filled out the questionnaire anonymously, and the interviewer read each question one at a time. Cooperation was excellent, and the variety of answers given provided good evidence that interviewer bias was successfully overcome. The key here was to utilize a self-administered questionnaire which guaranteed privacy while still retaining the advantage of the interviewer's presence.

The Telephone Interview

Most people own telephones in North America with the result that telephone contact is possible. Outside of North America, however, the situation is different. Consider, for

---

[5] "The Brazilian Evangelical," Bethany Fellowship (Wheaton Communications Research Report #41, April, 1975).

example, the percentage of households with telephones in Europe:[6]

Sweden	90%
Switzerland	88
Denmark	54
Netherlands	43
U.K.	34
W. Germany	31
Italy	27
France	19

In the developing countries, only the most wealthy would have a telephone.

Another problem is the availability of up-to-date directories. Only the United States maintains accurate current listings.

Finally, people frequently are unwilling to talk with a stranger over the telephone. This can be overcome if a letter is sent to the household in advance advising that an interview will take place on a given date. This step, however, increases both the costs and the time required to complete the survey.

Direct Mail

Two obvious assumptions underlie the use of direct mail: (1) a literate population and (2) the availability of an accurate mailing list. Both of these become highly uncertain once one departs beyond the borders of the developed countries. Reported levels of literacy, by the way, can be misleading. This may mean only that people can read at a primary level. Functional or working literacy may be much lower.

There are times when it will be impossible to gain an accurate mailing list. What is the source, for example, of all listeners to a missionary short-wave radio station within a given country? While there may be a small list of those who have

---

[6]Paul H. Berent, "International Research is Different," in Edward M. Mazze (ed.), *1975 Combined Proceedings* (Chicago: American Marketing Association, 1975), p. 295.

written in, this usually is not representative of the total listenership.

On the other hand, a mailing list may be readily available. Most organizations maintain an up-to-date list of donors and nondonors, and it is easy to draw an accurate sample from such listings. Under these circumstances, the direct mail approach probably is the ideal method.

To Sum Up

After objectives have been established and data requirements clarified, the next step is to decide upon the general type of research design. Should data be collected through observation, survey, or experiment? If a survey is to be utilized, should it be done in person, over the telephone, or through direct mail? These decisions always are made on the basis of a careful weighing of the pro's and con's attendant to each method. There is no such thing as an ideal design, and the final outcome always will be a compromise.

For Further Reading

Backstrom, Charles H., and Hursh, Gerald D. *Survey Research.* Evanston, Ill.: Northwestern University Press, 1963, ch. 1 (Planning the Survey).

Boyd, Harper W., Jr., and Westfall, Ralph. *Marketing Research: Text and Cases.* Homewood, Ill.: Richard D. Irwin, Inc., 1972, ch. 3 (experimentation) and ch. 4 (methods of data collection).

Campbell, Donald T., and Stanley, Julian C. *Experimental and Quasi-Experimental Designs for Research.* Chicago: Rand McNally & Company, 1963.

Erdos, Paul L., and Morgan, Arthur J. *Professional Mail Surveys.* New York: McGraw-Hill Book Co., Inc., 1970.

Ferber, Robert (ed.). *Handbook of Marketing Research.* New York: McGraw-Hill Book Co., 1974. Part B (Surveys).

Webb, Eugene J., Campbell, Donald T., Schwartz, Richard D., and Sechrest, Lee. *Unobtrusive Measures: Nonreactive Research in the Social Sciences.* Chicago: Rand McNally & Company, 1966.

Worcester, Robert M. (ed.). *Consumer Market Research Handbook.* London: McGraw-Hill Book Co., Ltd., 1972. Section 1 (collecting the data).

4

The Sample

Now we have reached the point of consideration of the first of the major methodological considerations in surveying — design of the sample (step 4 in Figure 3). Generally it is not possible to study every audience member, with the result that a subset or sample must be chosen logically for analysis. Sampling is a complex subject, and this chapter can only serve as a general nonmathematical introduction. Enough is said here to enable the reader to tackle some of the simpler sampling problems, but it frequently will be necessary to consult an experienced researcher or statistician. There also are a number of useful reference books cited at the end of the chapter.

Some Basic Sampling Concepts

Probably the most basic question is, "Why sample at all?" The most obvious reason simply is the economic impossibility of contacting a large group of people. In reality, sampling is a common everyday phenomenon. The housewife examines two or three oranges to determine if others in the bin are fit for consumption. A few minutes of a television program are watched to evaluate whether further viewing is warranted. Thus, sampling is undertaken for the most common sense of reasons.

While sampling theory is based on some pretty complex mathematics (probability theory), the basic concept is not difficult to grasp. Let's assume that a church of 6000 members is in the preliminary stages of planning for a new building. The pastor asks, "I wonder if most people will go along with the Board on this?" Rather than talk with all 6000, it would be more sensible to focus on just a small subset or sample, say 500. Perhaps the names of every member of the congregation could be written on pieces of paper and placed in a large fish bowl. The bowl then is shaken until we are sure that the names are well distributed throughout the container. Then we would be safe in drawing out 500 names, one at a time, until the number of 500 is reached. There is every reason to assume that these 500 would be a good representation of the total. If we chose fewer names (perhaps just a handful) we could not be as certain of this fact. Furthermore, drawing great numbers of additional names probably would not add much to the accuracy of the data, although it would add to both the time and cost of the research.

The central question now pertains to the extent to which it is possible to generalize results from a small sample to the larger group from which the sample was chosen. Is it possible that a sample of 500 is a good cross section of all people in a church of 6000 members? The answer is found in the statistical theory of sampling. In brief, it can be shown that a sample will provide an accurate picture of the larger body *within measurable error limits if the sample is properly chosen.* It is recognized that no subset ever perfectly mirrors the whole. It will deviate in some way. But, if we can keep the deviation to a minimum and measure the extent of that deviation, then the data drawn from a sample will be very useful. This deviation is referred to as *sampling error,* and it can be minimized and measured if certain procedures to be discussed later are followed.

The Concept of Representativeness

The foundation requirement of all sampling is that the subgroup chosen be *representative* of the total population (or universe). In other words, our sample of 500 should be a picture of the whole church in miniature. Otherwise, there is no use in sampling at all. Each of the methods discussed in this chapter will meet this criterion if they are followed correctly.

The Concept of Randomness

The statistician would go one step beyond representativeness and say that the sample should be chosen by *random* means. Usually this is referred to as a *random sample*. To the average person this might imply that we can go out on the street and speak to the first people we meet. But there is a vast difference between haphazardness and randomness. A sample is said to be random only when *every* person in the total population has a known and equal chance of being selected. This was the situation when we chose our 500 names out of the 6000 in the fishbowl. In this sense, a random sample would be representative, but the reverse is not necessarily true unless certain precise procedures are followed.

Why is randomness so important? The reason is that one cannot generalize from the sample to the total population within measurable error limits unless randomness is guaranteed. It is the underlying requirement of what is known technically in sampling theory as statistical inference. Without this information, we could be way off in our estimates without even knowing it.

The statistician begins by asking two important questions. First, how precise do you want your estimate to be? Or, to put it in different terms, how much statistical error is allowable in your sample — 1 percent, 5 percent, or what? This is a managerial question, not a statistical one. Assume, for example, that our intent is to estimate the listenership to a new Christian radio program. It will not be necessary to have a highly precise estimate in order to decide whether or not to continue the program on the air. In other words, we can tolerate some error in the sample estimate. Perhaps we might be satisfied if we can say with confidence that actual listenership falls in the interval of our survey estimate (say, 17 percent) plus or minus three percent. We could thus conclude that true listenership is some-where between 14 and 20 percent. If we had set our initial listenership objective at 10 percent, then this would be a clear indication that we have been successful. A more precise esti-mate would have demanded a more costly, larger-sized sample, and it would have been unnecessary.

Next the statistician will ask, how confident do you want to be that the true value actually lies within the error limit (techni-cally referred to as a confidence interval) that you have chosen? For instance, do you want to be 50 percent confident, 90 percent confident, or 95 percent certain that the true listener-ship falls in the interval of 14-20 percent? Again this is a man-agerial decision. Obviously we will want to be pretty certain of that estimate if we are to base a decision on these results. Generally management will say that we want to be 95 percent certain, and we thus establish what is known as the "95 percent confidence level." More technically, this says that the actual value in the population will fall within the specified error limit in 95 out of 100 samples chosen by the method used. We are only running a 5 percent risk that we have an erroneous estimate. We can reduce this risk even further, but the costs of larger samples which are necessitated can become astronomical.

To review, a sample estimate never will precisely mirror the true value in the total population, but we can arrive at an estimate of that value within known and measurable error limits. We must specify in advance how much statistical error we will tolerate and how confident we desire to be that we have arrived at a correct estimate. Once these decisions are made, then it is possible to evaluate the most appropriate sampling method and the required sample size.

Working It Out in Practice

The random sample represents the ideal. *One always strives for randomness* because of the ability provided to generalize from the sample to the population within the specified error limits. But, as later discussion will disclose, random sampling methods often are not applicable. Cost is a particularly potent factor. What does one do then?

It is important to recall that the foundational criterion is that the sample be *representative.* It can be representative, in turn, without being random. If we can ascertain that representativeness has been achieved, the data still are useful for managerial decisions. The price paid is that we cannot project our results to the target population or, as the statisticians refer to it, to the universe within the measurable error limits. Nevertheless, one can still assume that the sample is a good picture of the universe and make decisions accordingly. Certainly there will be some statistical error which remains unmeasured, but it is perfectly valid to project our sample results to the universe *managerially* as long as we are pretty sure the sample indeed *is* representative.

At this point the author has entered the battlefield between the statistical purist and the research practitioner. The purist tends to insist that samples must be chosen randomly if any use is to be made of the data. The applied reasearcher, on the other hand, realizes that the real world presents some significant barriers against the achievement of randomness. These will be stressed later in the chapter. In fact, one leading commercial researcher with his doctorate in research methodology recently told the Wheaton communication students that the random sample is a fiction in the real world. The most we can do is to strive toward this ideal but we must also realize that the world of reality and the world of the textbooks can be vastly different.

THE STEPS IN SAMPLING

There are four basic steps in sample design: (1) *definition of the group to be studied* (the target population or universe); (2) *determination of the source of names;* (3) *determination of sample size;* and (4) *selection of actual respondents.*

Definition of the Target Population

One of the recent projects in the Wheaton Graduate

School was determination of attitudes of members toward the missions program of the Presbyterian Church of America. This program is known as Missions to the World, and it represents a new thrust for this denomination. What is the target population? Perhaps pastors could provide the needed data and hence serve as accurate spokesmen for their congregations. If so, pastors would be specified as the target. More likely, however, it will be necessary to go directly to the laymen to find out their awareness, attitudes, and behavior. Laymen throughout the denomination (as contrasted with any given specific geographic area) were in fact selected as the primary target for this project, although pastors also were surveyed.

This decision cannot be made by a statistician. Executives themselves must specify the population after careful consideration of such questions as, "What do I want to know?" "Who can provide the information?" "How broad geographically should my inquiry extend — to all possible people or to some subgroup?"

Determination of the Source of Names

The next decision is to find a list of names of those to be contacted. Continuing with the above example, there is no single list of names of all laymen at the denominational office. Therefore, the sample initially must be churches chosen at random throughout the denomination. Specific names, in turn, must be chosen from the church rolls at the local level. Often the decision is much easier and the sample will be chosen from a mailing list, a telephone directory, a map of homes in a village, and so on.

Determination of Sample Size

The methodology for determination of sample size finds its roots in statistical theory and hence can become quite complex. The general principles are not difficult to grasp, however. It must be assumed that the degree of allowable statistical error and the desired confidence interval have been specified. There now are many formulae which can be utilized to compute the sample size, although many of these have been reduced to some rather simple tables.

Let's return to the example of congregational awareness and attitudes toward Missions to the World. Assume, for purposes of this handbook, that management is willing to accept an error of 5 percent and a confidence level of 95 percent (the actual decisions made in this project were different). The table in Figure 7 now can provide a good estimate, and the sample size which emerges is 384. It should be pointed out here that this is the sample size required for what is known as the "simple" or "unrestricted" random sample, a term which will be defined and elaborated upon below. In actual reality the Missions to the World project required a larger sample, but this example illustrates the thought process involved.

ERROR WHICH CAN BE TOLERATED	DESIRED CONFIDENCE	
	95%[a]	99%[b]
1%	9,604	16,587
2%	2,401	4,147
3%	1,067	1,843
4%	600	1,037
5%	384	663
6%	267	461
7%	196	339

Figure 7. A Guide to Estimation of Sample Size[1]

Notice what happens when a more precise estimate (i.e., less statistical error) is specified. As common sense would suggest, a larger sample is required. Furthermore, a higher

[1]Derived from Mildren Parten, *Surveys, Polls, and Samples: Practical Procedures* (New York: Harper, 1950), pp. 305-19.

[a] 95 out of 100 samples will reflect the total population within the error range

[b] 99 out of 100 samples will reflect the total population within the error range

degree of confidence from 95 percent to 99 percent leads to dramatic increases in the sample size.

The table in Figure 7 obviously is not complete. It gives the results derived from statistical formulae for only a few combinations of error and confidence. Most of the books referred to at the end of the chapter will be of further help. But in the final analysis it often is necessary to consult someone who has studied statistics and knows how to apply this theory to practical problems.

There is another limitation to the table in Figure 7, and it was alluded to briefly in reference to the Missions to the World example. It assumes that the population being studied is homogeneous. It is more likely in complex problems that there are groups or *strata* within the population which differ in known ways. Obviously a sample should be chosen from each of these groups to be certain that the results are representative. In such instances, referred to as *stratified sampling,* the resulting sample size probably will be larger.

There are other factors to consider when estimating sample size. One concerns the realities of data tabulation. Often it is desired to segregate the sample into various subgroups so that responses can be compared for differences. Age, for example, may be related to missions awareness, in which case it will be necessary to *cross tabulate* all of the awareness and attitude answers by age so that any resulting differences can be analyzed. This simply means that the answers will be analyzed separately within each age group. If the total sample is small to begin with, there may be too few in a given subcategory (say, the number in the age category 55-64) to allow for a meaningful analysis. This in itself would call for a relatively large sample regardless of statistical consideration. Generally speaking, samples of 400 or more allow for this kind of analysis.

The last consideration often is most important — cost. Assume that it will cost $5.00 apiece for individual personal interviews in the Missions to the World study. A sample of 384 would thus require $1920 for interviewing alone. Now, what must happen if the total allowable budget for the project is $1000? It will be necessary to cut costs somewhere. One obvious solution is to interview by direct mail, which, in fact, was the approach used in that survey. But if personal interviews are felt to be necessary, the only alternative is to reduce sample size. Refer back to Figure 7 and see what will happen if sample size is reduced to 200. We now have raised our error range somewhat to 7 percent, assuming no change in the 95 percent confidence level. Missions to the World executives must ask if this much error is allowable. Most likely it would be, but it now will be more difficult to cross tabulate the data extensively. Yet, we may have no choice simply because of financial realities.

Sample size, then, requires a tradeoff between three considerations: (1) statistical precision (allowable error and confidence level); (2) tabulation requirements; and (3) costs. One cannot increase statistical precision without increasing costs.

It might be of interest to note that most of the studies undertaken at the Wheaton Graduate School have utilized sample sizes of at least 350 whenever possible. One qualitative survey consisted of indepth interviews with only 50 people. On the other hand, nearly 5000 Christians were interviewed in the study of the church in Brazil. This was a complex stratified sample in seven cities within several major denominations. The 300-400 minimum thus is only a rough guideline. Generally samples of that size offer sufficient statistical precision and tabulation advantages without being unduly costly.

Selection of Respondents

The final step is actual selection from the list of names of those to be interviewed. This can be done either by probability methods which are designed to draw a random sample or by nonprobability methods. These two major approaches, probability and nonprobability, are discussed in the next two sections of this chapter. Once again it should be stressed that randomness is an ideal to be strived for. Often it is not attainable in practice. The most important consideration is representativeness, and all of the methods discussed below are designed to achieve this objective.

SELECTION OF RESPONDENTS:
PROBABILITY METHODS

There are three basic random sampling methods: (1) *the simple random sample;* (2) *the stratified random sample;* and (3) *the area cluster sample.*

The Simple Random Sample

Assume that it is desired to begin a new evangelistic outreach person-to-person among freshmen students at a major university and that it is felt desirable to measure attitudes toward Christianity before the program is launched. The first step would be to find a name list. Perhaps there are 1000 freshmen and our research plan calls for a sample of 200. It now will be necessary to number each student from 1 to 1000, and there are a number of ways in which we can draw 200 at random. Remember that the objective is to insure that each has an equal chance of being selected.

In this case we will be drawing a simple or, more technically, an *unrestricted* random sample. This approach is based on two assumptions; (1) the availability of a list of names and (2) homogeneity within the list itself. The latter assumption requires that there not be major differences between people on the list which would require segregation into strata, each of which should be sampled in and of itself. Undoubtedly the freshmen would be sufficiently homogeneous on the subject of religion to permit avoidance of this design complexity.

One common selection method is to utilize a table of random numbers, a portion of which is reproduced in Figure 8. This table may appear confusing at first, but all it consists of is numbers listed without any internal ordering. One can select any 200 four-digit numbers off this list and be absolutely certain that randomness will be attained.

58

	1	2	3	4	5	6	7	8	9	10	11	12	13	14	15	16	17	18	19	20	21	22	23	24	25
1	0	0	8	3	6	8	1	6	8	4	4	7	8	0	1	3	3	6	7	3	0	5	6	0	7
2	2	6	4	1	9	5	4	5	3	4	4	2	6	0	0	8	0	7	6	9	8	7	7	0	0
3	5	7	8	3	7	0	9	7	6	3	2	3	7	9	8	2	3	1	9	7	0	9	7	1	9
4	5	0	4	3	7	0	0	2	6	4	8	2	1	3	7	6	4	6	9	9	4	5	3	1	7
5	2	1	3	5	2	1	9	6	2	2	0	3	7	5	9	1	8	9	7	0	3	1	4	0	6
6	0	0	9	1	0	4	9	3	8	8	7	8	9	5	1	5	0	1	6	2	1	3	1	1	2
7	5	7	5	8	0	4	2	2	2	0	2	6	2	9	1	0	6	1	0	3	0	8	5	6	2
8	9	0	3	0	8	8	2	3	5	1	3	1	0	4	3	6	9	3	5	0	4	0	0	5	9
9	6	4	4	5	6	5	7	6	4	5	1	2	9	6	0	2	1	6	9	5	4	5	1	0	4
10	4	2	4	2	8	8	2	3	5	1	6	0	0	5	8	0	3	9	3	6	1	3	0	0	8
11	1	0	8	9	3	0	3	0	7	4	6	2	4	1	8	4	9	3	4	4	9	7	1	0	4
12	7	3	4	6	3	2	4	3	3	7	8	8	8	6	5	2	4	2	6	9	9	7	3	4	8
13	5	0	5	6	0	0	2	8	5	8	0	0	7	7	8	2	3	9	9	5	1	7	0	3	6
14	3	8	5	5	6	8	7	5	9	9	0	9	9	8	3	7	9	7	8	7	6	7	9	3	0
15	5	0	6	5	6	7	4	3	2	7	7	5	3	0	0	4	4	6	7	8	8	8	7	0	4
16	4	6	0	8	5	8	9	4	8	0	0	2	9	0	7	5	1	5	9	3	4	5	6	0	9
17	9	0	2	2	9	7	5	4	1	9	7	6	3	3	7	2	7	4	6	6	9	4	8	8	5
18	0	2	1	1	2	5	5	6	7	6	1	4	8	2	4	3	4	9	7	9	5	7	2	5	6
19	2	6	4	4	5	0	2	0	8	1	6	3	1	5	2	0	9	5	7	0	9	0	2	1	8
20	7	1	7	4	7	3	4	0	4	8	1	7	0	6	0	8	7	2	7	0	8	9	0	5	3
21	4	8	2	4	2	5	6	4	6	9	7	2	5	7	5	2	5	0	9	1	1	9	7	4	8
22	2	8	7	8	3	3	1	8	5	5	6	8	3	4	6	5	6	7	0	5	9	2	8	3	0
23	3	6	1	5	2	9	2	9	2	6	5	4	9	0	5	3	9	5	6	8	2	1	6	1	8
24	9	3	6	1	8	0	9	1	1	0	0	6	0	1	4	1	0	8	4	9	1	3	8	9	1
25	5	7	8	9	4	0	5	8	3	1	9	6	5	4	9	8	2	9	3	1	1	2	4	4	4
26	7	5	8	6	9	5	3	3	9	3	1	8	7	3	4	3	1	3	4	2	3	3	7	1	9
27	1	6	1	5	7	3	1	7	6	1	8	4	3	8	0	4	2	1	3	3	7	4	1	6	4
28	4	9	9	5	3	4	9	0	5	3	8	2	7	4	4	4	1	9	9	6	8	7	8	1	5
29	2	3	9	4	5	1	1	0	6	6	2	8	3	7	8	9	3	1	8	9	6	8	4	5	0
30	4	1	3	6	8	4	6	4	5	3	9	5	6	6	2	9	3	3	7	4	6	1	2	7	6
31	5	9	6	6	5	5	1	4	6	1	3	2	6	2	3	8	2	2	9	8	7	6	7	4	0
32	6	7	6	5	7	2	2	0	1	0	0	4	0	7	6	7	8	9	2	6	7	7	5	7	4
33	9	6	6	0	0	8	5	4	8	9	5	1	2	2	7	1	6	2	1	8	4	3	8	9	3
34	9	4	5	6	0	3	1	5	1	8	6	8	8	9	1	0	2	8	0	3	6	5	7	4	1
35	6	8	8	0	4	4	8	7	7	8	4	4	0	0	0	3	4	5	7	7	7	5	9	5	6
36	2	6	7	3	9	4	9	4	1	3	6	7	1	3	7	8	5	9	5	0	7	7	4	1	5
37	8	2	9	3	6	4	8	7	4	4	7	8	7	3	1	4	5	1	0	3	9	8	9	6	7
38	0	1	3	1	7	9	4	0	7	4	8	1	5	7	3	0	7	8	3	3	8	7	5	4	8
39	4	2	0	7	8	4	4	8	8	8	1	7	6	5	6	3	9	5	0	4	3	1	5	9	5
40	3	6	4	3	5	5	3	8	6	6	3	7	4	8	4	8	9	3	5	2	8	9	2	1	3
41	8	6	1	6	1	9	9	5	4	0	7	0	2	6	3	0	2	3	9	4	8	9	2	0	4
42	9	9	3	4	1	6	5	3	7	9	1	3	4	8	9	3	7	6	4	5	6	8	5	5	8
43	5	4	7	8	6	3	2	9	7	1	3	1	9	3	1	0	7	2	2	1	8	5	0	3	6
44	9	1	8	1	9	6	6	5	3	6	7	7	7	1	1	1	2	7	7	9	2	3	0	8	4
45	2	7	1	2	6	2	6	1	5	0	8	8	4	2	9	1	4	6	0	2	5	8	9	7	2
46	1	0	5	1	2	2	6	1	1	2	6	1	4	0	1	3	8	0	3	8	0	0	4	1	0
47	0	5	9	9	7	3	9	2	4	0	7	5	3	3	2	9	4	5	0	0	7	4	2	2	8
48	8	7	6	8	8	1	7	2	6	4	5	3	3	3	6	7	5	3	5	2	9	5	2	6	3
49	0	6	4	6	1	9	6	2	6	2	5	7	2	2	1	0	6	0	5	6	9	5	6	2	1
50	2	9	5	6	2	9	3	7	0	3	7	5	7	2	0	1	0	7	6	0	0	9	1	9	8

Figure 8. Table of Random Numbers (1)

Just for convenience, let's begin in the upper left-hand corner of the table of random numbers. Actually one can start anywhere. We must choose 200 four digit numbers between 0001 and 1000. The first number encountered is 0083 (row 1, columns 1-4). We now can move in any direction and select another number between 0001 and 1000, assuming, of course, that it has not been chosen before. The next number encountered moving down the page is 0091 (row 6). After the 200 numbers are chosen, then the corresponding names are taken off the freshmen list.

This method can become quite laborious, especially if the sample is large. A more convenient approach is *systematic sampling*. The first step is to divide the number on the total list by the number desired in the sample. In the example of our freshman class 1000 divided by 200 would equal five. In systematic sampling we now can go through the list and pick every fifth name and still have a randomly chosen sample of 200. Randomness is retained by guaranteeing that the starting point between one and five is chosen randomly. All one need do is to refer to the table of random numbers again and select a digit in the interval of one to five. Again, one may enter the table at any point. The author entered the table at the intersection of row 31 and column 11 and selected the digit "3." This means that the first name chosen will be the third on the list, and the second will be number eight, and so on.

It is obvious that systematic sampling can be a great timesaver. Because of this advantage, it probably is the most utilized of all random sampling methods when up-to-date lists of names are readily accessible.

The Stratified Random Sample

Assume now that a list of names is available but that it contains heterogeneity. Now it will be necessary to segregate the list into subgroups or *strata* and chose a sample from each. This is the meaning of the term stratified sampling.

Suppose that there are only 75 women in the freshmen

class and that there is good reason to believe their attitudes toward religion differ from their male counterparts. A sample of 200 chosen by systematic means could easily undersample or oversample the women. To avoid that error men and women will be placed on individual lists with a separate sample chosen from each. Thus, each is treated as a stratum of the total. Usually the total sample will be allocated in the proportion that these strata represent in the total population, although there are cases in which a disproportionate allocation is made for technical statistical reasons beyond the scope of this book. In this case women represent 7.5 percent of the total class. They also must represent 7.5 percent of the sample of 200 or a total of 15.

Stratified sampling often is required in survey work. For example, the author's colleague on the Wheaton staff, Dr. Donald Miller, undertook a survey among church members in Nigeria to assess their responses to the *African Challenge* magazine and other related issues.[2] Miller rightly suspected that responses would differ according to denominational background, even though all of the church members were located in the metropolitan area of Lagos. A list of all churches was compiled and 20 were chosen for this study stratified by denomination in the same proportion as these denominations appeared in the total population of churches. Names then were chosen from the church rolls, and a total of 997 usable questionnaires were obtained. If the sample had not been stratified, it is doubtful that the denominational variations would have been adequately represented.

The Area Cluster Sample

It is not uncommon to encounter a research problem in which there is no list of names and the population is dispersed geographically. The latter problem, in particular, will call for a way of reducing interviewing costs. The area cluster sample is the most logical approach under these circumstances, because

---

[2]Donald Miller, "How to Publish in Nigeria for Nominal Christians in Churches" (Sudan Interior Mission Communication Center, May, 1973).

it confines interviewing to a limited number of areas. This type of sampling can become quite complex, although the fundamental concepts are not difficult to grasp. The reader should note, however, that a statistically trained consultant should be utilized.

Two examples will help illustrate this method. Missionary radio station ELWA retained Daystar Communications, Inc. to survey its English language listening audience in Monrovia, Liberia.[3] Not surprisingly, there is no single list of Monrovia residents, and this almost always is the case in any large city. Furthermore, the city encompasses a wide geographic area. The basic approach was to divide the city map into 650 plots through a grid imposed on the map. Of these plots, 23 were chosen at random as sample clusters. A total sample of 4,952 adults and children was interviewed, with the sample size within each plot roughly proportional to the population itself.

The report of the ELWA study does not specify how individual respondents were chosen within the plot. At times it is possible to assign a number to each dwelling unit and select those to be interviewed from a table of random numbers. Another approach is to begin at one of the four corners of the plot, with the starting point chosen at random. Then dwelling units are interviewed systematically from that point on. For example, every sixth home might be chosen moving in a particular direction. This latter approach, for the most part, is confined to the United States and western European countries in which homes are laid out in orderly fashion.[4] Such neighborhoods in the developing countries often are more helter skelter than orderly, with the result that systematic selection of respondents can become nearly impossible. In such circumstances, recourse often is made to the quota sample method discussed below.

[3] "The English-Speaking Radio Audience of Liberia" (Conducted for Radio ELWA by Daystar Communications, Inc., 1970).

[4] For a detailed yet easy-to-follow description of this sampling procedure, see Charles H. Backstrom and Gerald D. Hursh, *Survey Research* (Evanston, Ill.: Northwestern University Press, 1963), ch. 2.

To take another example, the Ministry of Education of the Government of Ecuador and the United States government represented by USAID cooperated in a survey of the Quechua Indian population of Ecuador. The purpose was to facilitate the design and development of a bilingual education program. The sampling problem was a demanding one indeed, because little was known about these highly inaccessible communities. Dr. Ted Haney of the Far Eastern Broadcasting Company served as a primary consultant and designed a multiple stage area sample. The Quechua population first was divided according to provincias (states), and then by cantones (state sub-divisions), parroquias (counties), and communities. The final sample consisted of 24 communities and a total of 650 personal interviews within these 24 communities. Before individual dwellings could be chosen, however, the interviewer had to map each village. Then the homes to be interviewed were selected from a table of random numbers. The number of interviews in each community ranged from 10 to 30.

Again, it should be stressed that the steps in this type of sampling can be demanding if any semblance of randomness is to be achieved. Usually a trained consultant will be required. Fortunately, most of the research problems encountered by the Christian communicator can be tackled without recourse to such complex samples.

A Final Word on Randomness

There are many reasons why the final sample can deviate from true randomness, even though exacting sample designs are followed to the letter. Technically, for example, everyone chosen must be interviewed without substitution. Common sense would indicate that this rarely happens. One cannot call back indefinitely when the person chosen is not at home. Furthermore, a refusal to cooperate cannot be overcome unless one has access to some type of unusual coercion. Therefore, the resulting sample will never be perfect. It is in this sense that the commercial researcher referred to earlier stated that a random sample outside the world of the textbook is a fiction. These problems become compounded many times over in the developing countries.

What does one do, then, when the sample falls short even though the methods have been followed rigorously? Some purists will blanch at this statement, but many of those in applied research simply will *assume* that the sample is random if all evidence seems to indicate it is truly representative. This is not as dangerous a step as it might appear, because one could legitimately tolerate some deviations and still have a highly acceptable representative sample. Assuming it is random allows one to utilize a whole set of statistical procedures discussed in a later chapter designed to measure the extent of statistical error and so on.

SELECTION OF RESPONDENTS: NONPROBABILITY METHODS

Nonprobability methods make no attempt to achieve randomness. There is a price paid through the resulting inability to generalize data to the target population within measurable error limits. This does not invalidate this approach, however, in that representativeness, the cardinal criterion of a good sample, still is the goal. There are three commonly utilized methods: (1) *the convenience sample;* (2) *the purposive sample;* and (3) *the quota sample.*

The Convenience Sample

At times the research problem calls only for a quick indication of the audience situation. There may be neither the time nor the resources for a more systematic effort. A sample then would be chosen on the basis of quick availability of respondents and convenience to the researcher. For example, they might be recruited from those who pass on the street or who appear at the local market. The advantage is instant availability of respondents at very low cost. The method is not as haphazard as it might appear, for every effort still is made to insure that the sample is representative.

The convenience sample frequently is employed for purposes of pretesting. Here the objective is to assess potential response before a program is aired or a magazine printed. Experience has demonstrated that for purposes of pretesting about as much can be learned from a small convenience sample as from much larger randomly chosen samples.[5]

The Purposive Sample

There are times when the objective is to attain a preliminary measure of awareness, attitude, or behavior from widely dispersed respondents without recourse to some form of area sample. Sampling units thus will be chosen by the researcher on the basis of the judgment that they will adequately represent the population as a whole. For want of a better term, this is referred to as purposive sampling.

To take an illustration, the Evangelical Foreign Missions Association (EFMA) was vitally concerned about awareness and support for the cause of foreign missions within local churches in the United States. There was no funding for a full national sample. Instead, recourse was made to a purposive sample of ten carefully chosen churches.[6] A field executive of the National Association of Evangelicals, one of the members of this research team, selected these ten on the basis of his personal knowledge of United States churches, and the result was a diverse cross section. Later studies have indicated that these preliminary data gave a remarkably accurate picture, even though the sample was far from definitive.[7]

---

[5]See James F. Engel, Hugh G. Wales, and Martin R. Warshaw, *Promotional Strategy,* 3rd ed. (Homewood, Ill.: Richard D. Irwin, Inc., 1975), ch. 14.

[6]"Missions Attitude Survey," EFMA (Wheaton Communications Research Report #20, May, 1974).

[7]Various studies have been made of the awareness, attitudes, and behavior of the clientele of mission boards, and the results have closely paralleled the EFMA pilot survey.

The Quota Sample

The researcher often will know the characteristics of the target population in advance such as age, income, and sex. It thus is possible to select a representative sample by ensuring that the people chosen to be interviewed are in equal proportion to these characteristics. The selection of actual respondents is up to the interviewer, and the only requirement is that he or she fulfill the quota given in terms of age, sex, or other characteristics. In many ways this is similar to the stratified random sample, but the difference enters in that interviewers never are given this latitude in the latter approach.

Quota samples often are used in the developing countries in which the mechanics of random sampling become nearly impossible. The *Living Bible* was tested for its comprehensibility in Argentina through a quota sample based on age and education.[8] The quota was chosen as follows:

15-24 years of age and 7-10 years of education

37.5%

25 years of age and older and 7-10 years of education

37.5%

15-24 years of age and 11 or more years of education

12.5%

25 years of age and older and 11 or more years of education

12.5%

Each interviewer was given about ten questionnaires at a time to complete. Instructions were to interview a person who met the specified age and education criteria. The interviewer was at liberty to chose the person providing the respondent was a national, a non-Protestant, and not a relative or personal friend. Distant acquaintances could be interviewed, however. Actual interviews usually were obtained in parks, on the streets, on campuses, or in homes.

While a good cross section can be attained through this

---

[8]"Spanish Manuscript Evaluation for Living Bibles International, Latin American Phase" (Daystar Communications, Inc., November, 1975).

method, there always is concern over the latitude given the interviewer. There is a great temptation to select only those who are most available, regardless of their characteristics. The key to sampling accuracy when using quota samples thus lies in proper selection, training, and motivation of the interviewer.

SOME SAMPLING PROBLEMS

Handling "Not at Homes" and Refusals

No matter how carefully the sample is chosen, everything can break down if people either are not at home or refuse to answer the questions. There always will be a certain percentage who fall into these categories. One alternative is to call back at the home if the person is not available. Usually not more than one or two callbacks will be feasible because of cost. The other alternative is to select a sample initially which is larger than the intended final number, with the expectation that substitute names will be required. Finally, some researchers allow the option of interviewing a neighbor when the person either is not at home or refuses to cooperate. In a large sample, the effects on representatives and randomness will not be serious when this latter method is used, assuming the total of those chosen in this manner does not exceed 15-20 percent of the total.

Problems of Direct Mail Response

Direct mail research offers its own set of problems. Usually the sample design will not be difficult in that a systematic sample can be drawn from a readily available mailing list. But what happens when only a small proportion actually return the questionnaire? Some are more apt to reply than others, and the resulting sample can be quite a distortion of the target population. Furthermore, unduly lengthy questionnaires discourage response.

Generally, researchers aim for a 50 percent return as a minimum. The assumption is that a return of this magnitude will provide an adequate cross section. There are a variety of procedures which can be followed to increase return rates.[9] First, some type of initial contact with the respondent is helpful. This can be either through an advance letter, a telephone call requesting cooperation, or a statement of endorsement by a respected local official. Then it helps to print the questionnaire rather than to mimeograph or offset it in typescript. Response also seems to increase if the questionnaire is sent in a personally addressed hand-stamped envelope. Finally, it is advisable to provide some type of incentive. This could be an inexpensive curio or souvenir. The author has been hesitant to do much in the way of incentives in Christian direct-mail research, however, for the reason that it can seem inconsistent with the image the organization is attempting to project. If all else fails, return rates may increase if a second questionnaire is sent.

There are times when all the above methods will fail. There are two primary reasons. First, the mailing list itself may be poor. One of the early Wheaton research studies was undertaken to determine the attitudes of donors and non-donors toward a certain mission board. Just over 20 percent replied, in spite of the fact that all the above methods were utilized, except an incentive. Mission executives later explained that everyone who had any kind of contact with the mission whatsoever was placed on that list, regardless of their interest, and that list had not been carefully maintained. In retrospect, it is surprising that the return rate was not even lower.

Returns will be low also when respondent interest in the subject is not high. This often is the case in commercial product research. The only recourse in such situations is to use an attractive incentive, but then one cannot help wondering why people reply. Is it simply to acquire the incentive? If so, the validity of responses becomes suspect.

---

[9]An especially valuable resource is Paul L. Erdos and Arthur J. Morgan, *Professional Mail Surveys* (New York: McGraw-Hill Book Co., 1970). See also Eli P. Cox, III, Thomas Anderson, Jr., and David G. Fulcher, "Reappraising Mail Survey Response Rates." *Journal of Marketing Research,* vol. 11 (November, 1974), pp. 413-17.

The Sample

What does one do when return rates are low? The only advice is to use caution in interpretation of results. One never has the luxury of discarding the findings, although the temptation to do so may be high. The only reasonable alternative is to glean everything possible from the study in spite of the fact that it falls short of the methodological ideal.

Sampling in the Absence of Trained Researchers

It frequently has been stressed that complicated sampling plans cannot be executed without training and expertise. What does one do when trained people are not available to serve as consultants? One good suggestion is to avoid extensive geographic samples. One can learn a great deal by interviewing within just a few churches in the local area, and it may not be necessary to go beyond these boundaries. Furthermore, nonprobability methods usually will be a good substitute for more complex random sampling plans. Always remember that representativeness is the goal. A managerially useful representative sampling plan is within the ability of most readers of this handbook. Simple random samples, especially using the systematic method, also can be undertaken without much background or expertise.

To Sum Up

Usually it will not be possible to survey everyone in a target population, with the result that some type of sample becomes a necessity. The objective is to draw as accurate a cross section of this universe as possible. Ideally this is done through probability methods which guarantee that everyone has an equal chance of being selected. This will result in a random sample from which it is possible to generalize from the sample to the target population within measurable error limits. Various nonprobability methods also will result in a representative sample, but there is loss of this ability to generalize within measurable limits. Nevertheless, nonprobability methods will result in managerially useful samples as long as one does not insist on being a methodological purist.

We have discussed various methods, and all can result in useful samples. But as in every other phase of research design, there always is a tradeoff between the ideal and the realities of the situation. Substantial compromise can be made as long as one does not sacrifice the all-important criterion of representiveness.

For Further Reading

Backstrom, Charles H., and Hursh, Gerald D. *Survey Research.* Evanston, Ill.: Northwestern University Press, 1963, ch. 2.

Boyd, Harper W., Jr., and Westfall, Ralph. *Marketing Research: Test and Cases.* Homewood, Ill.: Richard D. Irwin, Inc., 1972, chs. 8 and 10.

Churchill, Gilbert A., Jr. *Marketing Research: Methodological Foundations.* Hinsdale, Ill.: The Dryden Press, 1976, chs. 8 and 9.

Ferber, Robert (ed.). *Handbook of Marketing Research.* New York: McGraw-Hill Book Co., 1974. Part C.

Kish, Leslie. *Survey Sampling.* New York: John Wiley & Sons, Inc., 1965.

Worcester, Robert M. (ed.). *Consumer Market Research Handbook.* London: McGraw-Hill Book Co. Ltd., 1972, ch. 3.

5

Designing the Questionnaire

After sampling decisions have been made, the next logical step in the research process (Figure 3) is to design the data collection instrument, although in reality the sampling plan and this step may be undertaken simultaneously. In survey work, the questionnaire is the basic tool of data collection.

The questionnaire is nothing more than structured, goal-oriented communication. The greatest difficulty with a questionnaire is to minimize that ever-present problem of bias — *the errors and mistakes made in the communication process which cause the findings to deviate from the truth.* Bias can never be eliminated completely, because questionnaire design still is more of an art than it is a science. Yet, there are some common-sense rules which, if followed, will reduce bias to acceptable levels and result in useful research findings.

It is good to recognize at the outset that most of the published manuals on this subject assume that the population is literate and resides in North America. Unfortunately, a good many of the rules of practice which seem to work in that setting are not applicable elsewhere. Therefore, the so-called "established" design procedures must be extensively adapted and modified when applied outside of North America. Every effort must be made to provide some practical insights into this adaptation process. In the final analysis, however, no handbook can provide clues for every situation. Therefore, the reader should anticipate the necessity of testing and experimentation.

This is the first of two chapters on this subject. This chapter is confined to general principles of questionnaire design, whereas chapter 6 focuses in more depth on approaches used to measure attitude, awareness, life style, and so on.

THE QUESTIONNAIRE DESIGN PROCESS

Questionnaires never can be designed by any formula, because questionnaire construction, as with all other forms of communication, requires the use of creativity. The obvious starting point is to become thoroughly immersed in the objectives of the project. Exactly what information must be gathered? If there is any fuzziness here it will be reflected also in the questionnaire itself.

The next step, frankly, is to engage in creative brainstorming. There are many ways to ask the same question, and each may be equally effective. The best practice simply is to "let the creative juices flow." The rules of thumb presented in this chapter will be of help here, but they can only serve as rough guidelines.

Once the questionnaire is constructed, it must be pretested. The reason is to ascertain whether respondents understand the questions and will answer as intended. The ultimate criteria of a workable questionnaire are twofold: (1) all research objectives are covered by the questions and (2) the instrument communicates as intended and elicits the desired response.

The Four Basic Types of Questions

Figure 9 provides a simple diagram of the basic categories of questions.

	Structured	Unstructured
Undisguised	1	3
Disguised	2	4

Figure 9. Four Variations of Question Design and Structure

Structure refers to the presence or absence of response alternatives. If categories of response are provided, the question is said to be structured, and vice versa. The criterion of disguise, on the other hand, designates the extent to which the real purpose of the question is obvious to the respondent. An undisguised question comes right out and asks for the desired information, whereas a disguised question will employ various means to get at the information.

The Structured, Undisguised Question (1). Here is an example of a question which falls into this category:

> Do you feel that your church needs more or less congregational singing during the Sunday morning worship service? (check one)
> ____ Needs more
> ____ Needs less
> ____ Neither more nor less
> ____ No opinion

This type of question is easy to administer in the field. Only one response is possible, and no difficulties are presented for an interviewer (if one is utilized). Moreover, the presence of structure provides a distinct advantage in ease of tabulation. It is a simple step to move from the questionnaire to a mechanical tabulation without the time-consuming intervening stage of careful checking and interpretation. The widespread utilization of computers in tabulation and analysis calls for the use of structured questions whenever possible.

This format also presents some disadvantages. First, it cannot reveal the reasons for the response without additional probing questions. The respondent is not allowed to use his or her own words, and significant nuances may be lost in the process. Furthermore, the undisguised format can, in some circumstances, make the respondent hesitant to reveal true feelings. This is especially likely in the developing countries in which a prevailing "people orientation" often leads the respondent to reply in terms he or she feels an interviewer wants to hear. The actual true response can be something quite different.

A final disadvantage is known as "order bias." This is observed most often in the form of a tendency to check the first response provided, regardless of true feelings. This is especially prevalent in the yes/no type of question. Some people always say yes, and this factor has led the author to avoid yes/no questions if the intent is to uncover attitude or intensity of opinion. Order bias can be minimized by scrambling the listing of response alternatives from one questionnaire to another, but such a step often serves only to compound the difficulties in tabulation.

The Structured, Disguised Question (2). The advantages of structure can be retained while minimizing reluctance to reveal true feelings in response to a direct question. Wording can be varied to allow the person being interviewed to reply in such a manner that he or she will not readily perceive the real intent of the question. One common procedure is to ask the question in third-person form as the following example illustrates:

> Would you say that most of the people in your church would prefer more or less congregational singing during the Sunday morning worship service? (check one)
> ____ Prefer more
> ____ Prefer less
> ____ Neither more nor less
> ____ No opinion

The assumption of the third-person format is that the answer given will, in reality, reveal the respondent's own opinions. Presumably the question will not be perceived as threatening and hence will elicit a more accurate reply. This assumption has never been verified conclusively in a North American setting, but this fact does not, in itself, invalidate the approach. The author has interacted with many who feel that it is a helpful alternative in attitude measurement in the developing country. Often one must resort to a variety of questioning formats to overcome the danger of eliciting only the "expected" and socially acceptable answer.

The Unstructured, Undisguised Qusstion (3). This type of format omits response alternatives and lets the respondent use his or her own words. Our question now might be worded in this way:

> What are your feelings about congregational singing during the Sunday morning service? Would you like more singing, less singing, or what?

After the response is given the interviewer then is free to probe with additional questions such as "Why did you say that?" "Can you tell me more?"

This free-response format is useful in several circumstances: (1) when there is no advance knowledge about the answer categories respondents will use; (2) when there is great variability in replies from one person to the next; (3) when there is a desire to avoid structuring thinking so as to elicit the respondent's own words which then will be followed by probing for clarification; and (4) when there is a desire to probe more deeply into underlying motivations and reasons.

As would be expected, there also are some disadvantages. An interviewer must be utilized if probing is desired, and the cost factor increases. Next, the interviewer must record responses verbatim, and this places obvious demands on interviewing skill. Third, the format still is undisguised and reluctance to reply truthfully is not necessarily overcome, although the use of probes is an advantage. Finally, tabulation and analysis are more difficult. There are some ways to tabulate open-end responses mechanically, but they increase expenditures of both time and funds in the research process. In spite of the disadvantages, the quantity and quality of data yield frequently are offsetting facts.

The Unstructured, Disguised Question (4). This type of question opens the door for almost unlimited creativity and variety in format. It now is possible to utilize the whole range of

Figure 10. A Pictorial Projective Question

"projective questions."[1] Sometimes these are in pictorial form such as the example in Figure 10. Notice that one person makes a statement about the need for more congregational singing. The respondent now is asked, "What do you think the other person will say?" Presumably they will reveal their own attitudes and beliefs. Once again, there is no definitive proof that this, in fact, takes place. Also one should use pictorial formats with caution outside of North America because of widespread variations in visual literacy from one people to the next. It may be impossible for some to "project themselves" into something as abstract as a cartoon or drawing.

There are other versions of unstructured, disguised questions such as word association and sentence completion. Yet, the author is hesitant to expand this discussion in the absence of proof that such methods are more successful in overcoming bias than other alternatives. Those who are interested in exploring this discussion further are encouraged to consult the references cited at the end of the chapter.

Concluding Comments on General Format. Most researchers are in agreement that structured questions do offer the advantage of greater ease of tabulation, although the data yield from unstructured questions often is greater. Whether or not some measure of disguise is introduced depends upon the sensitivity of the subject matter and the willingness of those being interviewed to reply openly and honestly. Unstructured questions generally are limited to those areas in which it is necessary to probe further to achieve greater depth and/or clarity in response.

Some Guidelines for Questionnaire Construction

While there is no simple formula to follow, there are some rules of thumb which will prove helpful both in design of one's

---

[1]See, for example, Harper W. Boyd, Jr. and Ralph Westfall, *Marketing Research: Test and Cases,* 3rd ed. (Homewood, Ill.: Richard D. Irwin, Inc., 1972), ch. 14.

own questionnaire and in evaluation of those designed by others.

Do the Questions Relate to Stated Objectives? One of the most frequent errors is to load a questionnaire with interesting but basically irrelevant queries. The fundamental criterion in evaluation of each question is, *how will this information be of value in planning?* In other words, does the data fulfill the objectives stated for the research project or are we engaging in the luxury of collecting unnecessary information?

Each of the research objectives ideally is fulfilled by utilization of two or more questions. The reason for this is that any single question may be invalidated by bias. Two or more measures which indicate convergent replies, however, are a good indication that the information is valid. This is done often by alternate questions spaced throughout the questionnaire.

Does the Respondent Actually Have the Information? Here is a question which may appear to be quite innocuous:

> What is your opinion of the tax reform legislation now being considered by Parliament?
> _____ I am in favor of it
> _____ I am opposed to it
> _____ I am neither in favor nor opposed
> _____ I am not sure

Most people will give an answer, and the data then will be duly tabulated and reported. Thus, the question has been successfully accomplished with entirely fictitious replies and the data are, of course, completely meaningless. No doubt people will reply for a variety of reasons. Some actually may believe they have heard of such legislation and hence should have an opinion. Others will answer something to save face and appear knowledgeable.

The obvious conclusion is that one never can assume that a person has knowledge on a given issue. The best strategy is to begin with questions such as these before asking for their opinion: "Have you heard anything about the tax reform legislation now being considered by Parliament?" (If yes) "Do you remember any of the details?" If accurate answers are not given, questioning should cease, and vice versa.

Is the Flow of Questions Logical? Always bear in mind that a questionnaire is basically nothing more than structured conversation. One rarely jumps back and forth in disjointed fashion in normal day-to-day conversation; yet this is a common mistake in questionnaire design. The result is failure to develop a logical and consistent thought pattern.

First, great care must be devoted to the introduction. It must be worded so as to create a favorable impression. It is especially important to establish the credibility of the research sponsor and the interviewer as well. Here is an example of one well-worded approach:

> Hello. I am a student at the University. We are taking a survey on some of the issues people in your neighborhood are talking about these days. Could I have about fifteen minutes of your time now? Or, if you are busy right now, could I come back later?

Here the credibility of the sponsor is established immediately. The introduction does not reveal the specific purpose of the survey. If people are aware of the purpose and/or the sponsor they could easily bias all the answers given. Finally, it states the amount of time which will be required and evidences a willingness to return if that would be more convenient.

There are many other variations which can be utilized to secure respondent cooperation, and this subject is discussed in more depth in chapter 7. The important point to stress now is the necessity of beginning on a positive footing. One seldom can recover unless rapport is established at the outset.

The first few questions after the introduction usually should be neutral. Visualize an inverted funnel and you will grasp the significance of this approach. We start with broad and general stimuli and gradually work toward the specific and more sensitive issues. One could start, for example, by asking "How long have you and your family lived at this address?" This information may be completely irrelevant to the research objectives, but it does serve to initiate the questioning process.

Always be aware that once a question is asked on a subject all other related questions will be affected. It would be a grave error, for instance, to mention the name "Baptist" in early questions if the purpose of the project is to assess both awareness and attitudes toward the local Baptist church. It is much more sensible to focus on the church in general and then move gradually toward the specifics with respect to the local Baptist church.

A bias also is introduced if many yes/no questions are used consecutively. The respondent could check yes on a few initial questions and continue doing so because of the yeasayer/naysayer bias mentioned earlier. Variations in question format will help.

The questionnaire generally is concluded with classification questions — age, income, education, and so on. Some make the mistake of placing them at the outset on the assumption that they are neutral and nonthreatening, whereas the reverse is more likely to be true. Age and income, in particular, are sensitive items of information which will be revealed with accuracy only when real rapport has been established between interviewer and respondent.

One aid in logical questionnaire flow is to preface obvious breaks in subject matter with some form of transition statement. When this occurs it is wise to insert a phrase such as "now shifting a bit to another issue," and so on.

Does the Subject Matter Require More Than One Question? The inexperienced researcher frequently attempts to ask too much in one question. The following example is not unusual:

> When you attend the Sunday evening service at your church, would you say that it generally meets your spiritual needs?

First, it is assumed that the respondent actually attends evening services, and this must be verified with a preliminary question. Moreover, what would it mean if the person being interviewed simply replied yes? What does this answer say? No guidance is provided at all in assessing just what the respondent really likes and dislikes about the service. In reality there should be a battery of questions on this issue, each of which focuses on a specific dimension.

Are Questions Worded Appropriately? There are three common problems in wording: (1) *ambiguity;* (2) *misperception;* and (3) *loading.*

(1) Ambiguity. Words such as "generally," "usually," and "often" are indefinite. The question on Sunday evening church attendance for example, inquired whether or not the Sunday evening service *generally* met spiritual needs. There can be variability from one service to another, and recall is limited primarily to those which are most recent. Therefore it may be more appropriate to focus on what happened within the time period of ready recall, generally the most recent occasion.

There are other ways in which ambiguity can be a problem. Consider this question: "Would you say that your pastor's sermons are helpful?" What does *helpful* mean? One person might reply that a sermon is helpful if it keeps him awake. Another might be helped only if there is guidance provided in biblical exegesis. Still others interpret this term to refer to the extent to which practical issues in life were addressed. The only way to introduce clarity is to attach specific referents such as "helpful in meeting the problems you have in daily living" and so on.

The only way to detect ambiguity is through pretesting! A small group of people should be asked to indicate exactly what the question said to them. The researcher should not be satisfied until everyone gives the same meaning.

There are times when ambiguous wording is intentionally utilized to introduce a subject. For instance, it would be legitimate to begin by asking "Would you say that your pastor's sermons are helpful in meeting your spiritual needs?" This question in and of itself will not reveal much, and it might not even be tabulated. The real meat is provided by following questions which focus in on the specifics.

(2) Misperception. Words frequently lie outside the experience of the respondent and hence have no real meaning. Rural black adults in the Southern United States were asked many years ago if they favored governmental control of profits. Responses were decidedly negative, because many appeared to feel that "prophets should be regulated only by the Lord."[2] While this example is now mostly of historical interest, it certainly illustrates the point that one never should assume that words will be understood. The researcher in Christian communication, in particular, should avoid theological terms such as "spirituality," "justification," and "salvation" unless it has been determined by pretesting that those being interviewed have a working knowledge of the meaning of these words.

(3) Loaded Questions. A question is loaded when the wording favors one answer over another. Usually this mistake is made inadvertently, but some unethical researchers will deliberately load a question to prove a point. Whatever the reason, it violates the criterion that questions must be *neutral* in wording.

Let's examine some loaded questions, a few of which are quite subtle:

Many are saying that the decision of the Board of Elders to air-condition the sanctuary is unnecessary this year. Do you agree or disagree?

2) In view of the teaching in Romans 13 on support of the civil government, do you agree that hippies and other long-haired protesters should be jailed?

3) Many of the liberals and neoevangelicals no longer believe the Word of God. In view of this, we have decided to use only

2Quinn McNemar, "Opinion-Attitude Methodology," *Psychological Bulletin,* Vol. 36 (1946), p. 317.

the King James Bible in our worship. Do you support this policy or not?

4) Billy Graham recently published a new best seller on the Holy Spirit. Have you read it yet?

5) Did you attend church last Sunday?

These examples may appear to be extreme and contrived, but the author has encountered many just like them in nearly two decades of research experience. Each is seriously loaded. Notice in the first question that the case has already been stacked by the notation that many are opposed to the elders' decision. This, in itself, will predispose some to side with the crowd and also voice their opposition. If one wants to support his or her own viewpoint in such a controversy, this is a good way to go about it. In so doing, however, research has departed from its role of objective information gathering.

The second illustration uses some emotionally charged words — "hippies" and "long-haired protesters." All kinds of negative images are thus connoted. In addition, a biblical passage is quoted which easily can be misinterpreted if not taken in the context of the whole counsel of the Word of God. Many thus would agree that these people should be jailed, whereas they might have taken a different position if the loaded words had been removed.

The third question also uses some horrendously loaded terms and makes a sweeping statement about biblical inspiration which, at best, is only a half truth. Then the King James Version is presented in that context as the only alternative. A valid response is unlikely.

The last two questions are much less obvious. On the surface it seems harmless to ask whether or not one has read Billy Graham's latest book. Bias enters, however, by using the name of a prestige figure and the word "best seller." Some would be hesitant to say no simply because they would not want to admit to anyone that they had been "negligent." In this instance, it would have been better to ask initially if the respondent had heard of Dr. Graham's latest book. In the event of a yes reply, questioning might proceed this way: "What is its title?" "Have you read it?" "What would you say was the most valuable thing to you personally about this book?" Notice that this would make it much more difficult to give a false positive claim of readership.

The last question seems to be the most innocuous of all, but it too stacks the case in the direction of a positive answer. Many will be hesitant to admit that they missed church out of fear that the interviewer will evaluate them negatively. If questions are asked in this way, the accuracy of the claim always should be verified by probes on the sermon title and so on.

There are times when loaded questions are deliberately used, and this is when a battery of stimuli is presented to probe aspects of life style. This subject is explored in depth in the next chapter, but to provide a few examples respondents often are asked whether or not they agree or disagree with these kinds of statements:

> If people would work harder and complain less, this would be a better country.
>
> Improving the welfare of people is more important than increasing our national defense budget.
>
> Organized religion should deal more with social problems.
>
> When I play a game or a sport, my technique is more important than winning or losing.

Such statements obviously are provocative, but the intent is to induce the respondent to take a stand and reveal his own opinion. Usually a variety of such statements will be used, and there will be more than one stimulus on each issue. The respondent is instructed to state exactly how he or she feels in each case. Experience to date, especially in North America, has confirmed that this type of questioning seems to be valid, and it has found widespread use in marketing research.[3]

Is Respondent Fatigue Likely? The author often is asked to indicate how long a questionnaire should be. Probably the best answer is to quote Abraham Lincoln when he was asked how long a man's legs should be. Lincoln replied, "just long enough to reach the ground." Brevity is a virtue, however, in reducing respondent fatigue, data processing, and analysis and interpretation.

There is a point at which respondent fatigue can enter. There is no way to detect this limit other than to pretest the questionnaire and observe what happens. People usually will protest if it is unduly lengthy. The key variable is the degree of interest the person evidences on the subject under examination. One Wheaton Graduate School project focused on alternatives to children's television programing.[4] Parents and children alike were asked to evaluate the programs directed to this audience segment. Parents, in particular, proved to be most anxious to talk about this subject which has been of growing concern in many North American families. The interviews could have been extended for hours if the research team had so desired. In other instances, just a few questions will prove to be too many because of disinterest.

Using These Guidelines. It must be stressed once again that questionnaires are not designed by formulae. At best the above suggestions are rules of thumb to be modified as circumstances warrant. Furthermore, there are vast crosscultural differences which simply cannot be addressed in a brief handbook. Therefore, the reader should use what is said here only as a starting point and verify the appropriateness of the resulting questionnaire by pretest.

---

[3]See William D. Wells (ed.), *Life Style and Psychographics* (Chicago: American Marketing Association, 1974).

[4]"Alternatives to Children's Television" (Wheaton Communications Research Report series, still in preparation).

Pretesting the Questionnaire

The pretest really is the only basis upon which to determine the extent to which a questionnaire actually communicates as intended. This need not be a costly or time-consuming project. As a general rule, pretests start with about ten people who represent a good cross section of the target population. The questionnaire is administered under actual field conditions. Then the respondent is asked to indicate, for each question, exactly what was being asked. If some deviation is found from the intended content, wording changes are made on the spot. Then the corrected version is tested on the next person. This is continued until it is apparent that all questions perform as intended. Generally this process can be accomplished with no more than twenty people. At times, however, two or more pretests will be necessary to produce an adequate data collection instrument.

It also is helpful to ask those in the pretest for their suggestions in wording. This often proves to be a real help in "fine tuning" the instrument.

There will never come a point at which the researcher has sufficient experience with a particular format to make the pretest unnecessary. The author has found that deficiencies always enter every time he has failed to pretest. Unfortunately these shortcomings are discovered after the fact rather than before. Therefore, at least a small-scale pretest always should be undertaken.

Physical Layout of the Questionnaire

The actual layout of the questionnaire is also an important consideration. It is necessary to comment briefly about (1) *the printing process;* (2) *the provision of instructions;* and (3) *tabulation considerations.*

Printing

In the more developed countries, it generally is advisable to set the questionnaire in type or have it printed by offset from carefully typed copy. Mimeograph or ditto tends to create a bad impression. In other situations, however, the reverse might be true. The determining factor is the extent to which the appearance facilitates rather than inhibits response.

Provision of Instructions

A good rule is never to take anything for granted and to place complete instructions right on the questionnaire. Personal interviewers, for example, must be reminded where to probe, how to vary the order of questions, and so on, to avoid the inevitable mistakes which otherwise will be made.

Careful attention to instructions becomes even more important when self-administered questionnaires are utilized. Here is a question from a direct-mail questionnaire which is part of a series focusing on felt needs:

Having a happy home (check only one)
_____ I really need help here
_____ I would like some help here
_____ This isn't much of a problem for me
_____ This is not a problem for me

The reader may be surprised to learn that many people will check more than one response category unless directed not to, and even the presence of instructions is no guarantee that just one reply will be given.

Frequently it is necessary to repeat instructions again and again. One church familiar to the author asks missionary support candidates to fill out a detailed questionnaire. In one section these candidates are asked to indicate which of four types of possible ministry they will be undertaking. Then a series of questions is asked under the category chosen. Most candidates answered the questions for *all four ministries,* however, even though the instructions clearly called for something different. Obviously the instructions must be repeated at the outset of each of the ministry categories, warning the candidate that only one is to be chosen.

Tabulation Considerations

Complex questionnaires usually cannot be tabulated accurately by hand. Hopefully a computer will be available, but this is not always the case. In the absence of a computer, the Indecks punchcard system can be helpful.[5] This consists of a 5" x 8" punch card with eighty numbers around the outside. Each question is assigned a position on this card and a hole is punched to indicate the response. Tabulations then are made by hand counting those which are punched in a certain way. In addition, it is possible to separate subgroups and tabulate them separately.

The computer of course, represents the ideal. It utilizes an 80-column punch card. In addition, there are 10 possible numbers which can be punched in each column ranging from 0 to 9. Only one punch is allowed per column.

Reference to a carefully prepared questionnaire will help in discovering the manner in which one goes about transferring information from the instrument itself to the punch card and then into the computer (Figure 11). The objective is to assign each question to a column on the punch card. Then the various responses to that question are punched within that column, ranging from 0 to 9. Notice the small numbers at the far right-hand side of each question in Figure 11. These designate the punch-card column. Question 1, for example, appears in column 1. Then there are four possible responses to question 1, each of which is also designated by a number. If the person replied that he is a pastor, this would be punched as a "1" in column 1 and so on. If no response is given, this generally is entered as "0."

---

[5] Available through INDECKS Company, Arlington, Vermont 05250 USA

PRESBYTERIAN CHURCH IN AMERICA

Stewardship Survey, 1976

This is the Survey about which we recently wrote you. Your prompt attention to it will be deeply appreciated.

Please remember these things:

1. The Questionnaire is anonymous with no names attached. Therefore be very frank and honest in your answers.

2. Return it promptly in the enclosed self-addressed envelope.

3. The results of this Survey will help all of us in the P.C.A. Therefore we ask you to answer the questions fully and carefully.

Thanks so much for your cooperation.

★ | ★ | ★ | ★ | ★ |

I. First, we would like to know about your role in the local church and whether you receive certain literature published by the denomination.

1. Which of the following catagories best describes your status in your home church (check only one)?
1) _____ Pastor
2) _____ Elder
3) _____ Layperson
4) _____ Other (please explain) _____ (1)

2. In the past two months, have you received a copy of "Continuing . . .," the official news publication of the Presbyterian Church in America?
1) _____ Yes   2) _____ No   3) _____ I'm not sure   (2)
If "Yes", how much of the last issue did you read? (check one)
1) _____ All or most of it   3) _____ Skimmed it   (3)
2) _____ less than half   4) _____ None of it

3. The P.C.A's Committee on Stewardship publishes a periodic brochure entitled "Commitment." Have you received a copy within the past two months?
1) _____ Yes   2) _____ No   3) _____ I'm not sure   (4)
If "Yes," how much of the last issue did you read? (check one)
1) _____ All or most of it   3) _____ Skimmed it   (5)
2) _____ Less than half   4) _____ None of it

89

II. **As you know, the national level of the Presbyterian Church in America is comprised of four major standing committees. In the spaces below, please write in the names of as many of the four as you know.**

1) _____

2) _____

3) _____ (6)

4) _____

(After you have completed the above, do not change your answer later on as you finish the Questionnaire.)

III. **In the section below we have listed a number of factors that may or may not help you in deciding which Christian organization(s) you will support financially (including but not limited to P.C.A. causes). After each one, please check how important it is to you in making such decisions.**

	VERY IMPORTANT	IMPORTANT	SOMEWHAT IMPORTANT	NOT IMPORTANT	
The organization should adhere to and/or promote reformed theology.	1	2	3	4	(7)
The organization should be nationally known	1	2	3	4	(8)
The organization should have a history of careful use of the funds it receives	1	2	3	4	(9)

Figure 11. A Questionnaire Precoded for Computer Tabulation

Question 2 would require some editing whereby a notation is made for the keypuncher as to which of the correct answers is given. There are times in which it defeats the purpose of the questionnaire to provide the answer categories.

Question 3 begins a series of attitude questions. These also are physically laid out to facilitate computer tabulation. The keypuncher would simply punch the answer which is checked, ranging from 1 to 4.

90

There will be times in which multiple answers are allowable for a given question. Remember that only one punch may appear per column. This means that each answer must be assigned a separate column. If it is mentioned it is keypunched as an "1." Nonmention would be keypunched as a "0."

Sometimes two or three tabulating cards are required for long questionnaires. It is less expensive, however, to reduce the number of questions to eighty or less and thereby utilize a single card.

The advantage of structured questions should now be even more apparent to the reader. The questionnaire in Figure 11 is precoded and hence may be keypunched directly. This results in considerable reduction of cost and time expenditures. The layout itself, in turn, is critical. Answer alternatives should, whenever possible, be listed directly under the question and be clearly distinguishable for the keypuncher.

To Sum Up

The purpose of the first of two chapters on questionnaire design has been to expose the reader to the stages in the process and to present some general rules of thumb. Obviously questionnaire construction is more of an art than a science.

The goal always is to produce an instrument which meets the stated objectives in clear and logical fashion. The closer the questionnaire is to actual conversation, the better it is likely to communicate as intended. Bias is an ever-present dilemma, and the guidelines presented can be of help in avoiding some of the more blatant errors. The final determinant, however, always must be an actual pretest.

For Further Reading

Backstrom, Charles H., and Hursh, Gerald D. *Survey Research.* Evanston, Ill.: Northwestern University Press, 1963, chs. 3 and 4.

Churchill, Gilbert A., Jr. *Marketing Research: Methodological Foundations.* Hinsdale, Ill.: The Dryden Press, 1976, ch. 6.

How Can I Get Them to Listen?

Ferber, Robert (ed.). *Handbook of Marketing Research.* New York: McGraw-Hill Book Co., 1974. Part B, chs. 1-4.

Oppenheim, A. N. *Questionnaire Design and Attitude Measurement.* New York: Basic Books, Inc., 1966.

Tull, Donald S., and Alabum, Gerald S. *Survey Research: A Decisional Approach.* New York: Intext Educational Publishers, 1973, chs. 5 and 6.

6

Environmental Analysis, Pretesting, and Measurement of Effectiveness

Figure 2 outlined the six steps in the planning process: (1) analysis of the environment (especially the spiritual status of the audience); (2) establishment of measurable goals; (3) determination of strategy; (4) execution of strategy; (5) analysis of effectiveness; and (6) evaluation. Research enters at stage 1 (analysis of spiritual status), stage 3 (pretesting), and stage 5 (measurement of effectiveness). It is the purpose of this chapter to present an overview of questionnaire methodology required to acquire (this) essential information.

It should be stressed once again at the outset that there never is one definitive or correct approach to research. Rather, the reader should analyze the examples given here and adapt them whenever possible, to fit his or her own unique situation.

ENVIRONMENTAL ANALYSIS: SPIRITUAL STATUS OF THE AUDIENCE

A model of the spiritual decision process was presented in Figure 5. To assess where members of a given audience fall with respect to this model, four basic categories of information are required: (1) *awareness;* (2) *attitude;* (3) *life styles;* and (4) *decision-making style.*

Awareness of the Biblical Message

For successful evangelism one must have an understanding of the biblical awareness of those for whom the message is directed — in particular awareness and grasp of the truths of monotheism, the nature of man as a sinner, and the claims of Jesus Christ with respect to salvation and life itself. Acceptance of the Bible as the Word of God also is a key factor. For several years Viggo Sogaard and his colleagues in Thailand have utilized questions which center on each of these eighteen specific factors:[1]

1. Who is God?
2. Where is God?
3. Who is Jesus Christ?
4. How did the world begin?
5. Can you see God?
6. Does God have power over evil spirits?
7. Does God love you?
8. Can God hear you and answer you?
9. What is the difference between God and man?
10. What is sin?
11. Have all men sinned?
12. What is salvation?
13. Does Jesus have anything to do with salvation?
14. How can a man be saved?
15. Does Jesus love everybody?
16. What is the Bible?
17. What is a Christian?
18. Do you personally have to be concerned about God, sin, and salvation?

In actual practice it probably is not necessary to include all of these individual items, but it does provide a useful checklist.

Up to this point most of the Wheaton studies have measured awareness through use of multiple choice questions of the type appearing in Figure 12. This format has worked satisfactorily in the United States, Canada, and Ecuador, although a more unstructured approach may be more useful if one is working in

---

[1]Viggo Sogaard, *Everything You Need to Know for a Cassette Ministry* (Minneapolis, Minn.: Bethany Fellowship, Inc., 1974), p. 59.

Environmental Analysis . . .

other developing countries. In addition, other questions usually are inserted throughout the questionnaire to explore these issues from a different perspective. For example, respondents in Vancouver were asked whether or not they agreed with these statements:

> Most of the problems in the world today are caused by man himself
>
> I feel that education has most of the answers for moral and social problems
>
> To me, the Ten Commandments are still good rules for today
>
> Of all the different philosophies which exist in this world, there probably is only one which is correct
>
> I have read the Bible at least once in the past month

11. For each of the following, which statement would you say most closely describes your own belief?

a. (1) _____ I do believe that there is a God
   (2) _____ I do not believe that there is a God
   (3) _____ I do not know if God exists or not
   (4) _____ I used to believe that God exists but I don't believe it now.

b. (1) _____ God is of central importance to my life
   (2) _____ God is important, but I know little about Him
   (3) _____ God is of no importance to my life
   (4) _____ I don't know if God is important to my life or not
   (5) _____ Or would you say something else? (write in)

c. (1) _____ Jesus was God
   (2) _____ Jesus was just an ordinary man
   (3) _____ I don't know what kind of person Jesus was
   (4) _____ Or would you say something else? (write in)

d. (1) _____ The Bible is God's word and all it says is true
   (2) _____ The Bible was written by men inspired by God, but it contains some human errors

(3) _____ The Bible is a valuable book because it was
written by wise and good men, but God
had nothing to do with it

(4) _____ The Bible was written by men who lived so
long ago that it is of little value today

(5) _____ The Bible is a collection of myths and stories
that are no more true than modern fairy tales

(6) _____ Or would you say something else? (write in)

e. (1) _____ Religion is important for man today

(2) _____ Religion is not important for man today

(3) _____ Religion is just a psychological crutch

(4) _____ I don't know if religion is important for man
today

(5) _____ Or would you say something else? (write in)

f. (1) _____ No religions really lead to God

(2) _____ Some religions lead to God

(3) _____ All religions lead to God

(4) _____ Only one religion leads to God

(5) _____ I don't know if any religions lead to God
or not

(6) _____ Or would you say something else? (write in)

Figure 12. Multiple Choice Questions on Spiritual Awareness[2]

A good case can be made for unstructured awareness
questions. There is always the risk that provision of the alternatives could have the adverse effect of leading the respondent to
select those which represent the "expected" reply. Campus
Crusade has long used the following question as a lead into an
evangelistic presentation: "Who is Jesus Christ according to
your understanding?" It has worked quite successfully, and
there is no reason why this format could not be utilized if it
proved to be more helpful in generating response.

---

[2]Source: "Spiritual Status Analysis, Vancouver Teenagers," Leighton Ford
Evangelistic Association (Wheaton Communications Research Report #55,
December, 1975).

Attitude

This second set of questions focuses on how the respondent feels about his or her biblical knowledge and its most visible manifestations — the individual Christian and the church. Attitudes, then, are evaluative rather than factual, and attitude change often is the goal of evangelistic communication on the assumption that attitude change can precede behavioral change.

The measurement of attitude is an extraordinarily complex subject, and the literature is vast indeed. All of the sources cited at the end of this chapter will be of help to the reader who wants to inquire further. The discussion here can only be introductory.

Attitudes by their very nature often are strongly held, especially those on religion. The result is that respondents frequently are reluctant to reveal their true feelings. This is particularly likely to be true in some of the developing countries. In such instances it may be necessary to utilize a disguised format. An example might be, "How would you say most of your friends and relatives feel about the Christian church?" This unstructured form then could be followed up by probes for clarification.

North American attitude research typically has made use of a variety of structured, undisguised attitude scales. Questions of this type were utilized in the survey of Vancouver teenagers who were asked the extent of agreement or disagreement with the following questions:

God is not as important to me as He once was

In my opinion, Christianity has the answers for the problems of the world today

Organized religion should try to deal more with social problems

In religious matters, I would have to be called a skeptic or agnostic

The response scale was constructed in this manner:

Strongly agree
Agree

Somewhat agree
Somewhat disagree
Disagree
Strongly disagree
Doesn't apply

This same approach also worked well among teenagers in Quito, Ecuador (see chapter 9 where the Quito study is discussed in depth).

There are many ways in which the answer categories can be varied. Sometimes five-scale positions are used, and other times it may be reduced to two — agree or disagree. The advantage of the longer scale is the ability to differentiate between degrees of agreement and disagreement. As a practical matter, the author prefers using a six- or seven-point scale largely for the reason that most people will not use the extreme categories on the scale. In tabulation the strongly agree and agree categories are combined into one for purposes of data analysis, and the same is true of the two extreme disagree categories. In the process a seven-point scale becomes reduced to five. If one starts with five, this reduction then drops to three, and one loses much of the benefit of this type of scaling.

As one moves from a North American setting, there are inevitable modifications required in methodology. First, those who are raised with a western world view tend to think in a linear pattern of logic and hence can respond readily to the types of scales discussed here. Asians, on the other hand, find them utterly foreign to their way of thinking. They easily can hold what would appear to the westerner as mutually inconsistent patterns of belief. Some in other parts of the world, in turn, cannot make the subtle differentiation between categories of agreement and disagreement. The Brazilian, for example, tends to think in black and white terms and cannot readily reply to the more complex scale.

Attitude research methodology thus is largely a product of North America, at least insofar as the published literature. Its applicability elsewhere in the world usually will require extensive adaptation. Perhaps it is best to begin with disguised questioning. Whatever the case, the researcher never can be a slave to a favorite method which has worked in his or her home setting.

Life Style

Life style questions have three distinct foci: (1) *assessment of felt need for change in life itself;* (2) *documentation of specific needs;* and (3) *exploration of basic general motivations.*

Felt Need for Change in Life. A general principle of successful communication is to concentrate on those individuals or segments of people who are looking for change in their life pattern. Others have a closed filter at that point in time and hence must be regarded as a nonreceptive target. Adults in Vancouver responded freely to the following questions, each of which was accompanied by a seven-point scale of agreement or disagreement:

> I would say I am pretty satisfied with my life the way it is
>
> I feel a sense of purpose in my life
>
> Frequently I consider the possibility of doing something altogether different with my life
>
> There are times when I feel very lonely
>
> I have a growing concern that my marriage isn't what it once was
>
> Sometimes I feel that life has given me the short end of the stick

These questions were scattered throughout a much larger grouping of related questions, and the first three proved to be particularly revealing. Most of those surveyed responded consistently that they were satisfied with life as it is. There was little evidence of interest in change and in Christianity as an alternative. There were some who exhibited an opposite profile, however, especially those under twenty-five and the more affluent person over thirty who has found the lure of materialism to be wearing thin. These people then were made the target of concentrated evangelistic effort.

Specific Felt Needs. People respond best when communication is seen as being relevant to their felt needs. As was stressed earlier, this is used as the avenue for a focusing of biblical truth on the underlying spiritual dimensions of these needs.

With a nonsophisticated, semiliterate audience, it may be necessary to measure felt needs in a nonstructured manner. The felt needs of Christians in Nigeria were assessed through use of two general questions.[3]

> At the moment, what is one personal problem facing you? Write your answer briefly on the line below.

> What is another personal problem facing you? Write your answer briefly on the line below.

Answers were categorized after the interview itself in order to permit mechanical tabulation.

The general rule in questionnaire construction is to strive for structure whenever possible. The author and his colleagues have found that a listing of categories of needs accompanied by a simple response scale works well in a variety of crosscultural situations. Figure 13 contains the questions used for this purpose when surveying members of the church of Brazil in seven major cities. Most were at best semiliterate, yet they responded appropriately to this instrument which was, by the way, carefully pretested in advance. Notice the careful wording and detailed explanation which was provided. It was necessary at the outset to establish that it was acceptable to admit the presence of spiritual need. Next, instructions were given for use of the scale, and a simple example was included. Finally, interviewers were present to assure that this self-administered questionnaire was understood and utilized correctly.

---

[3]Donald Miller, "How to Publish in Nigeria for Nominal Christians in Churches" (Sudan Interior Mission Communication Center, May, 1973).

Environmental Analysis . . .

All of us have areas of need in our Christian life. Also, we all need help as we try to follow Jesus. What are some of the needs of your life? We need to know these things so that the church can do a good job of helping you. Remember, no one will ever know who filled out the questionnaire. Names are not used.

Here is a list of needs many Christians have. After each one, please put a check mark in the box which best describes your own need. If you really need help in that area badly, check the first box. If you want some help and the need is not too urgent; check the second box. If it isn't much of a concern, check the third box.

Let's try one to be sure we understand.

	I really need help here	I would like some help	This isn't much of a concern to me	This is of no concern to me
Learning to swim				

If you would really like help in learning to swim, check the first box. If you would like some help but it isn't too urgent, check the second box. If swimming is not much of a concern to you, check the third box. If learning to swim is of *no* concern, check the last box. Do you understand?

	I really need help here	I would like some help	This isn't much of a concern to me	This is of no concern to me
How to hold family prayer and devotions				
Handling sexual temptations				
Control of temper				
Learning to love others more				
How to tell others about Jesus				
Handling my finances better				
Being a Christian on the job				
Helping my children grow up as Christians				

101

	I really need help here	I would like some help	This isn't much of a concern to me	This is of no concern to me
Understanding Christians of other groups and churches				
Birth control				
Finding out my special function in my local church				
Learning to help other people solve their problems				
Being a Christian in the home				
Making more money				

Figure 13. A Scale Utilized to Assess Specific Felt Needs of Christians in Brazil[4]

At times a prevailing common pattern of felt needs can best be determined by a survey of people after they accept Christ. This was done in Japan through use of the following question (percentages of positive responses are given in parentheses):[4]

When you began your religious quest, did you have within you the desire to search after any of the following?

The meaning of life	(40%)
The way to live rightly	(40%)
True love	(37%)
Meaning of death	(20%)
Release from loneliness	(18%)
Understanding of the contradictions of life	(15%)
Understanding of fate	(15%)
Realization of who I am	(12%)
Christianity as a cultural benefit	(12%)
Other	(10%)

---

[4]"How Japanese Become Christians" (Second Interim Report of the Baptism Motivation Survey of 1973-74, Lutheran World Federation Office of Communication, Tokyo).

Environmental Analysis . . .

General Motivations. Much use is now being made in the secular world of questions which isolate fundamental activities, information, and opinions.[5] These are referred to as "AIO" questions, and the whole inquiry has come to be designated by the term "psychographics." The purpose is to "flesh out" the understanding of the motivations of the audience in order to make communication messages, symbols, and formats of maximum relevance to the target.

The most common approach has been to use an extensive battery of questions which explore a wide arena of basic feelings and motivations. It is not uncommon to utilize 200 questions or more. Then those statements which are most descriptive of the target audience are isolated through computer analysis of various subgroups within a sample. Figure 14 provides a small section of an AIO questionnaire of the type employed in secular marketing research with a literate North American target audience.

11. For each of the following statements, please indicate the extent to which *you personally* agree or disagree with that statement. "X" the box that best describes your feelings about the statement. If a statement does not apply at all to you, "X" the box under "undecided or no opinion." "X" One Box For Each Statement

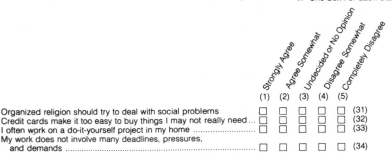

---

[5]For a full description of this methodology and its use in strategy, see William D. Wells (ed.), *Life Style and Psychographics* (Chicago: American Marketing Association, 1974).

103

How Can I Get Them to Listen?

	Strongly Agree	Agree Somewhat	Undecided or No Opinion	Disagree Somewhat	Completely Disagree	
	(1)	(2)	(3)	(4)	(5)	
I express my talents better in my leisure-time activities than in my job	☐	☐	☐	☐	☐	(35)
We do not often go out to dinner or the theater together	☐	☐	☐	☐	☐	(36)
Our family travels together quite a lot	☐	☐	☐	☐	☐	(37)
I would not like to have more leisure time than I have now	☐	☐	☐	☐	☐	(38)
Television is our primary source of entertainment	☐	☐	☐	☐	☐	(39)
Religion is more important to me today than it was five years ago	☐	☐	☐	☐	☐	(40)
On a vacation, I just want to rest and relax	☐	☐	☐	☐	☐	(41)
Using credit when you buy something is a bad practice	☐	☐	☐	☐	☐	(42)
When I play a game or a sport, my technique is more important than winning or losing	☐	☐	☐	☐	☐	(43)
A cabin by a quiet lake is a great place to spend the summer	☐	☐	☐	☐	☐	(44)
I will probably not have more money to spend next year than I have now	☐	☐	☐	☐	☐	(45)
I admire a successful businessman more than I admire a successful artist	☐	☐	☐	☐	☐	(46)
I hate to lose at anything	☐	☐	☐	☐	☐	(47)
People express their real self in their lesure-time activities	☐	☐	☐	☐	☐	(48)
I have more self-confidence than most people	☐	☐	☐	☐	☐	(49)
I am active in more than one service organization	☐	☐	☐	☐	☐	(50)
In the past ten years, we have lived in at least 3 different cities	☐	☐	☐	☐	☐	(51)
If people would work harder and complain less, this would be a better country	☐	☐	☐	☐	☐	(52)
Improving the welfare of people is more important than preserving wilderness	☐	☐	☐	☐	☐	(53)
I prefer to participate in individual sports more than team sports	☐	☐	☐	☐	☐	(54)
When it comes to my recreation, time is a more important factor to me than money	☐	☐	☐	☐	☐	(55)
I sometimes feel the presence of God	☐	☐	☐	☐	☐	(56)
Leisure means actively participating in various sports and games	☐	☐	☐	☐	☐	(57)
Five years from now, our family income will probably be a lot higher than it is now	☐	☐	☐	☐	☐	(58)

Figure 14 An Example of Secular Psychographic Research

This same general approach also is proving useful in research with Christian audiences. The intent is identical — to isolate those beliefs and motivations which describe members of the target audience. Experience at the Wheaton Graduate School thus far has indicated that it is not wise to use extensive batteries of questions and attempt to discover in the process of tabulation those which reveal target audiences. In other words, we attempt to utilize only those questions on which we have some reasonable assurance in advance that replies will have some usefulness in evangelistic strategy. Secular psychographic research, on the other hand, tends to be a kind of "fishing expedition" in which hundreds of questions are used in the hopes that a limited few will be useful later.

This type of inquiry proved to be useful in the study of Vancouver adults which was referred to earlier. The reader will recall that three groups demonstrated evidence of seeking change in life itself and hence were isolated as fruitful targets for evangelism. One of these consisted of adults over thirty who were earning high incomes. Specific felt needs and general AIO responses then were analyzed for these people in order to discover those dimensions on which they differ from people in general. First, they were found to be family oriented. Children and marriage were declared to be of basic importance, but both provide a source of worry. Marriages frequently were said to be eroding, and a felt need for help in this area loomed high. Moreover, they evidenced worry about the education of their children and their adjustment to life.

This group of adults also indicated a basic optimism about their ability to maintain a high standard of living. Yet, the husbands often voiced a felt need for help in finding job fulfillment. Finally, there was an openness to spiritual things. A large number replied with real interest in discovering the relevance of the Bible for life today. In short, this group is a prime target. There is every evidence that they can be reached by both mass media and personal outreach which provide solid answers to their concerns about family, marriage, and job fulfillment.

How Can I Get Them to Listen?

Psychographic research also is proving to be applicable in the developing countries if modifications are made. It was mentioned earlier that the Brazilian tends to think in black or white terms and has difficulty in replying in more subtle ways. General motivations were thus assessed by AIO type questions accompanied by a two-phase response scale. On the advice of a knowledgeable Brazilian anthropologist, respondents first were asked to read each question and to decide whether or not "this is me." Once that decision was made, they then were asked "How much is this me?" and vice versa.

They filled in a box which designated the appropriate response. This set of questions is included in Figure 15. Again, notice the careful wording of instructions and the inclusion of an illustration. All categories of response were used, and those interviewed did not reply only at the extreme points on the scale as feared. We have since used this same approach elsewhere with an equal degree of success.

Here are a number of statements which people often make about their interests, their needs, their goals, and those things which are important to them. You may feel that many also are true of you. Others might not be. What we want you to do is to read each statement carefully. Then we want you to tell us whether this is true of you. For example, a statement might read, "I like to eat popcorn," and you might say, "Yes, this is me." If you really like to eat popcorn and you strongly agree with that statement, take your pencil and fill in the big box closest to the left side. If you just like popcorn a little bit, fill in the little box. If you are kind of in-between, fill in the middle box. And you would do the same thing if you didn't like popcorn. Do you follow how we will answer these questions? Let's try one just to be sure. Here is a statement:

	This is me			This is not me		
I like to go swimming on hot days	☐	☐	☐	☐	☐	☐

Now, decide in your own mind, "This is me" or "This is not me." If you like to swim very much put a pencil mark in the big box on the left side under "This is me." If you just don't like to swim at all, mark the big box under "This is not me" (the box farthest to the right). If this statement is only somewhat true of you, that is, you just like to swim a little bit, mark the third

106

box or the smallest box under "This is me" and so on. Do you understand
now? Good.

	This is me	This is not me
I worry that I won't be able to give my children a good education	☐ ☐ ☐	☐ ☐ ☐
I like to pay cash for everything	☐ ☐ ☐	☐ ☐ ☐
There are times when I feel life has given me the short end of the stick	☐ ☐ ☐	☐ ☐ ☐
I find it pretty easy to accept change in most things	☐ ☐ ☐	☐ ☐ ☐
I have become well-enough acquainted with my three nearest neighbors that I know their hobbies or main interests	☐ ☐ ☐	☐ ☐ ☐
Within the past month I have invited a non-Christian into my home to visit	☐ ☐ ☐	☐ ☐ ☐
For me, Bible study is pretty much a daily thing	☐ ☐ ☐	☐ ☐ ☐
Compared to a year or two ago, I can see real growth in my Christian life	☐ ☐ ☐	☐ ☐ ☐
Within the past month I have tried to lead a non-Christian to faith in Jesus Christ	☐ ☐ ☐	☐ ☐ ☐
I am concerned that my Christian experience is up and down and not consistent	☐ ☐ ☐	☐ ☐ ☐
I feel I know how to confess and deal with sin in my life	☐ ☐ ☐	☐ ☐ ☐
I feel able to talk confidently with a non-Christian about his need of Christ	☐ ☐ ☐	☐ ☐ ☐
I would have to describe myself as a defeated Christian most of the time	☐ ☐ ☐	☐ ☐ ☐

**Figure 15. The Questionnaire Used to Measure
General Motivations of Brazilian Christians[6]**

[6]Source: "The Brazilian Evangelical," Bethany Fellowship (Wheaton
Communications Research Report #41, April, 1975).

Life style of the Local Congregation. All of the above questions can be utilized to evaluate a local congregation. One particular questionnaire, however, has been widely used for this purpose, and it is worthwhile to discuss it briefly. Designed by Indepth Evangelism Associates of the United States (IDEA), it is part of a total program which helps the church plan a strategy for both evangelism and cultivation (Figure 16).

IN-DEPTH EVANGELISM   CONGREGATIONAL SURVEY

SEX: Male ☐ Female ☐ │ AGE: Under 20 ☐ 20-34 ☐ 35-49 ☐ 50-64 ☐ 65 and over ☐

HOW FAR DO YOU LIVE FROM THIS CHURCH?
Less than ½ mile ☐ ½ to 2 miles ☐ 2 to 5 miles ☐ More than 5 miles ☐

HOW MANY SEPARATE SERVICES AND ACTIVITIES DO YOU USUALLY ATTEND EACH WEEK?
Less than 1 ☐ 1 ☐ 2 ☐ 3 ☐ 4 ☐ 5 ☐ Over 5 ☐ VISITOR ☐

	Yes	Not Really	Desire Change	Priority
1. Christ is so real to me that those at home, business and school can see the difference He makes in my life.				
2. I can tell of a specific answer to prayer within the past month.				
3. I take time for personal Bible reading at least three times a week.				
4. Praying together as a family is a part of our home life.				
5. Our church adequately "feeds" me spiritually and provides for continual growth in my Christian life.				
6. I don't just attend services but feel I am meaningfully involved in the life of our church.				
7. I have close friends in this church with whom I share personal feelings and concerns.				
8. I get together with a few Christians informally at least once a month specifically to share in prayer and Bible study.				
9. There is a positive spirit of oneness in our congregation.				
10. I am proud enough of our church that I feel free to recommend it to my closest friends and neighbors.				
11. I have become well enough acquainted with my three nearest neighbors that I know their hobbies or main interests.				
12. Within the past two months I have invited a non-Christian into my home to visit.				
13. I have a list of several persons for whom I pray specifically and regularly that they will accept Christ as Saviour.				
14. Our church demonstrates its concern for the people of the community by helping to meet some of the practical needs.				

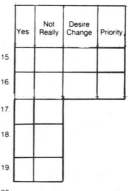

	Yes	Not Really	Desire Change	Priority
15. Within the past month I have tried to lead a non-Christian to faith in Jesus Christ. **15.**				
16. I feel *able* to talk confidently with a non-Christian about his need of Christ. **16.**				
17. I believe that a person who dies without receiving Jesus Christ as Saviour is eternally lost, even though he is a good, moral person. **17.**				
18. I believe that talking with non-Christians about their need of Christ is not only the responsibility of pastors and evangelists but *my* responsibility, too. **18.**				
19. I believe that we must *take* the gospel to those who do not attend church. **19.**				
20. If you were to die tonight and God should ask you, "Why should I let you into heaven?", what would you say? (Please write your answer.) **20.**				

Figure 16. The Indepth Evengelism Congregational Profile[7]

The questionnaire is administered in a Sunday service, and someone leads the congregation collectively question by question. Replies are completely anonymous. Questions 1-19 are answered "yes" or "not really." Respondents then are asked to review questions 1-16 and to check any of those areas in which they desire to see change in their own life. Then, these areas of change are ranked in order. Replies are segregated by age group, and the analysis reveals the most consistent felt needs for change within each group as well as the church collectively.

This instrument may have to be adapted to fit local circum-

[7]Source: Indepth Evangelism Associates (a ministry of the Latin American Mission).

stances. Its greatest asset is in collecting just enough data to enable a congregation to begin to develop a research-oriented strategy. In effect, it is best viewed as the starting point. A more extensive instrument probably should be utilized as the congregation becomes more adept in this way of thinking.

Decision Making Style

Attention now shifts to measurement of the influences on the decision itself, especially the effects of interpersonal influence and the mass media. Often one of the best research strategies is to focus inquiry on recent converts. This, of course, was the basic methodology of the Japanese study referred to earlier.[8] A total of 438 Christians responded to a highly structured questionnaire which assessed the relative influences of the church and Christian schools, Christian radio and literature, the role of personal witness of the minister and laity, and the influence of the family both in support and in opposition.

Media exposure information is of special importance in design of an evangelistic strategy, because the objective of media selection is to reach people where they are. The wording of these questions is identical to those employed to measure communication effectiveness, so further discussion is reserved for a later section in the chapter.

PRETESTING THE STRATEGY

A well-known pastor always evaluates his sermons in two ways prior to delivery: (1) they are given to his staff members and critiqued at least a week before the service; and (2) a small group of the congregation assembles for critique. In so doing he is able to assess comprehension of main points and the probable response. Needless to say, his preaching ministry has a far-reaching reputation for unusual clarity and power. This is what is meant by a pretest.

There are many approaches for pretesting, the most com-

---

[8]"How Japanese Become Christians."

mon being some type of recall test.[9] Members of the target audience are exposed under realistic reading or viewing conditions, and respondents are asked to play back what they heard. Also they may be asked to reveal the extent to which changes have taken place in attitude, intention, or behavior. Actual response is difficult to measure with any accuracy, however. Therefore, analysis of comprehension is the primary goal of the pretest.

Usually small samples are used for this purpose, ranging from 10 to 100. Convenience samples are most common, and the questionnaires are quite brief. Therefore, this type of research is usually inexpensive. Pretesting never guarantees the development of a "perfect" message, but it can sharply reduce the risk of failure. At the least, a poor message will be differentiated from an acceptable one. What cannot be done is to distinguish a good message from a great one, because the qualities which differentiate the two usually are subtle and nonmeasurable.

The benefits of pretesting were demonstrated conclusively in one Wheaton research project.[10] Spot radio announcements had been produced for airing over American Forces Radio and Television Service. The objective was to increase Bible reading and to encourage those in need of spiritual help to contact qualified counselors through a telephone hotline. It was suggested that these same spots would work with equal effectiveness with a general audience. Fortunately, a pretest was undertaken prior to the final decision.

The basic method was to contact approximately 100 members of the general public between the ages of eighteen and thirty-five. Announcements were recorded on cassettes with about thirty seconds of music before and after each spot to

---

[9]See James F. Engel, Hugh G. Wales, and Martin R. Warshaw, *Promotional Strategy,* 3rd ed. (Homewood, Ill.: Richard D. Irwin, Inc., 1975), chs. 13 and 14.

[10]"An Analysis of Project Linklines" (Wheaton Communications Report #29, July, 1974).

simulate the type of radio environment in which it might be aired. People were contacted in public places such as stores and train stations. Findings showed that very few of these spots were appropriate for general airing, and the outcome was a substantial saving of both funds and time which otherwise would have been largely wasted.

Pretesting is well within the means of any Christian organization. It should always be done even if the sample is no more than ten people. The gains in message comprehension, if nothing else, are well worth the effort.

MEASUREMENT OF EFFECTIVENESS

After the strategy has been executed, Christian stewardship requires some kind of effectiveness measurement. Communication impact can be documented in three ways: (1) *attraction of attention;* (2) *message reception;* and (3) *message response.*

Attraction of Attention

Attention attraction usually is measured by questions on readership or listenership. The methodology for this purpose is quite standardized because this type of research has been undertaken routinely by secular organizations since the late 1920s. Figure 17 contains one section of the questionnaire designed for this purpose by the Far Eastern Broadcasting Company. Notice that it starts general and then becomes quite specific with respect to program preference. Preferences are evaluated through open-end questions. This is a wise procedure because it avoids providing alternatives which might lead the respondent to check those programs which he or she thinks they "ought to hear."

Readership is evaluated in a similar way. Questions usually are confined only to the most recent issue of a periodical. Often the articles are listed by title, and respondents are asked if they "read all of it," "read some of it," "just skimmed it," or "didn't read it at all."

112

9. How did you find out about FEBC Manila or FEBA Seychelles? (Pick one.) told by a friend or relative _____ by accidently tuning in _____ by an advertisement or publication _____ other (Please specify.) _____ .

10. Approximately how often have you listened to FEBC Manila?
    almost daily _____ many times _____
    many times a week _____ a few times _____
    approximately once a week_____ once only _____
    once or twice a month _____ have never listened_____

11. Approximately how often have you listened to FEBA Seychelles?
    almost daily _____ many times _____
    many times a week _____ a few times _____
    approximately once a week_____ once only _____
    once or twice a month _____ have never listened_____

12. What kind of programmes do you listen to on our FEBC or FEBA station?
    sports_____ news_____ Christian teaching_____ variety_____ plays _____ devotional music_____ Indian film music_____ Indian classical music_____ Western folk music _____ Western popular music _____ Western classical music _____ other (Please specify.) _____

13. If you had time to listen to only one programme on our stations, which programme would you choose? (Please give the name of the programme or a description.).

14. If you had time to listen to two more programmes, which would they be? (Please give programme names or a description.)

15. If we wanted to change our programmes and introduce new ones, what suggestions could you give us? _____

16. What other shortwave foreign stations do you listen to? (Please list them in order of your preference.) _____

Figure 17. A Questionnaire Used to Measure Radio Listnership[11]

[11]Source: Courtesy of the Far Eastern Broadcasting Company

Message Reception

The primary measure of message reception is comprehension of its main points. Probably the simplest approach is to ask "What would you say was the main point of this article?" (or program, or sermon, and so on). An alternate approach is utilization of some true/false questions on actual content. Comprehension measurement, by the way, is always a verification of listenership or readership claims, which rarely should be taken at face value without some questions of this type.

Message Response

Response, of course, can be analyzed in several dimensions: (1) shifts in awareness; (2) changes in patterns of felt needs; (3) attitude change; and (4) behavioral change. Each of these outcomes should have been stated in the form of a measurable objective. Once that has been done it will be clear just what is required in the questionnaire designed for effectiveness measurement.

The project designed to reach high school youth in Quito, Ecuador (discussed in detail in chapter 9) was undertaken to attain the following types of goals:[12]

An increase from 53% to 68% of those who say that Jesus taught the way I ought to live.

An increase from 61% to 71% of those who say that God is important to me.

An agreement by 60% that Jesus offers help in coping with loneliness.

Recognition of the radio and newspaper theme "Algo Nuevo" (something new) by 70%.

An increase in the size of all participating church youth groups by 50%.

Three categories of goals are illustrated: (1) shifts in awareness

---

[12]"Algo Nuevo," HCJB (Wheaton Communications Research Report #58, December, 1975).

(goals 1 and 2); (2) need reduction (the third goal in which a stated percentage will associate the Christian answer with a felt need); and (3) church growth (an increase in the size of the participating churches).

Awareness and need-reduction goal attainments are measured by a readministration of the survey undertaken initially for purposes of analysis of spiritual status. Often the same people will be measured a second time in order to evaluate the extent of cognitive or behavioral shift. Another alternative is to utilize two carefully matched samples.

Church growth goals simply involve a tabulation of the numbers who appear on church rolls.[13] This is far better, by the way, than counting the number of so-called "decisions." There is increasing evidence that a recitation of the "sinner's prayer" is not a definitive indication that the person actually accepted Christ. A much better measure is proof that these same people become formally united with a church body and evidence signs of true spiritual growth.

It should be obvious by now that effectiveness measurement is impossible in the absence of precisely stated goals. Usually a goal will be stated in this way: "to impact society with the claims of Christ." This is nothing more than a broad statement of purpose or philosophy, and there is no way to assess actual achievements.

Classification Information

It is routine to collect classification information on all questionnaires. This consists of demographic data of the following types: (1) age; (2) sex; (3) social status; and (4) education. Other items which frequently are included are: (1) home ownership; (2) number of children; (3) church preference; (4) church attendance; and (5) participation in activities outside the home. The exact data included always varies from one project to another.

---

[13]A helpful manual for this purpose is Virgil Gerber, *God's Way to Keep a Church Going & Growing* (Glendale, Ca.: Regal Books, 1974).

How Can I Get Them to Listen?

These data are a major key to audience segmentation. How do younger respondents differ from older respondents? Does income make any difference in church preference? Are those with higher education less interested in spiritual things than those with less education? These kinds of questions are answered through a cross-classification analysis in which responses are segregated in terms of various audience subgroups so that comparisons can be made.

Demographic data also are helpful in providing a profile of those who respond. This is particularly helpful when the objective is to design a strategy to increase the financial contributions from supportive clientele. Strategies never can be very effective if one does not have a clear understanding of the characteristics of the target audience.

Figure 18 contains a page of demographic questions taken from a North American survey, and it is a good example of the standardized approach to demographic research. Notice that age and income are assessed in terms of broad categories. This is a great assist in overcoming reluctance to reveal this type of personal information.

VI. Now, some information about you. Please remember this is an anonymous survey so your answers are strictly confidential.

1. What is your age? (check one)
1) ____ Under 18	4) ____ 35-44	6) ____ 55-64
2) ____ 18-25	5) ____ 45-54	7) ____ 65 & over
3) ____ 26-34		(40)

2. Your sex: (check one)   1) ____ Female   2) ____ Male   (41)

3. Your marital status: (check one)
1) ____ Single   2) ____ Married   3) ____ Other

4. How many children do you have living with you? (check one)
1) ____ none	3) ____ two	5) ____ four
2) ____ one	4) ____ three	6) ____ five or more

5. How far have you gone in school? (check one)
1) ____ not a high school graduate

116

2) ___ high school graduate
3) ___ some college
4) ___ college graduate
5) ___ post graduate work

6. What is your occupation? (check one)
1) ___ pastor or full-time Christian worker
2) ___ Professional (physician, attorney, teacher, etc.)
3) ___ Business executive
4) ___ Office worker
5) ___ Housewife and/or mother
6) ___ Own a business
7) ___ Farmer/rancher
8) ___ Retired
9) ___ Other (please specify) _____ . (45)

7. In which state do you live? _____ (46)

8. In what type of area do you live? (check one)
1) ___ Urban area
2) ___ Suburban area
3) ___ Small town or city (which is not a suburb)
4) ___ Rural

9. Of all the money you contributed to Christian causes last year, what percent did you give to P.C.A. causes?
1) ___ less than 10%   5) ___ 40-49%
2) ___ 10-19%   6) ___ 50-64%
3) ___ 20-29%   7) ___ 65-79%
4) ___ 30-39%   8) ___ 80-100%

10. What is the yearly income of your household? (check one)
1) ___ under $5,000   5) ___ $15,000-$19,999
2) ___ $5,000-$7,499   6) ___ $20,000-$29,999
3) ___ $7,500-$9,999   7) ___ $30,000-$49,000
4) ___ $10,000-$14,999   8) ___ $50,000 and above

11. Church attendance: (check one)
1) ___ I attend regularly with definite church responsibilities (teach Sunday School, usher, etc.)
2) ___ I attend regularly with no definite responsibility
3) ___ I attend irregularly
4) ___ I do not attend more than 3 or 4 times a year

Figure 18. Analysis of Demographic Characteristics

117

The measurement of social status can be difficult. It is approximated by income levels, educational attainment, or occupation. One can utilize one or more of these questions depending upon the extent to which it appears that they, in fact, reveal social status. In a North American setting, occupation is no longer a very useful measure, and income also can be a misleading indicator. Education, all things considered, may be the best measure. Quite the reverse can be true in other environments. Again, adaptation is always the key to successful questionnaire design.

To Sum Up

This has been a lengthy chapter designed to provide illustrations of the basic principles discussed in chapter 5. A number of examples have been given of the ways to measure spiritual status (awareness, attitudes, life styles, and decision making styles), probable success of the communication strategy (pretesting), and actual effectiveness of the strategy. Once again it must be stressed that there is no such thing as *the* correct approach. The examples here should be viewed only as thought starters and idea generators. Borrowing someone else's efforts without proper adaptation and pretesting can be a fatal mistake.

For Further Reading

Ferber, Robert (ed.). *Handbook of Marketing Research.* New York: McGraw-Hill Book Company, 1974. Section III, Part A (behavioral science techniques); Section IV, Part C (advertising research).

Gerber, Virgil. *God's Way to Keep a Church Going & Growing.* Glendale, Ca.: Regal Books, 1974.

Oppenheim, A. N. *Questionnaire Design and Attitude Measurement.* New York: Basic Books, Inc., 1966.

Shaw, Marvin E. and Wright, Jack M. *Scales for the Measurement of Attitudes.* New York: McGraw-Hill Book Company, 1967. (Contains many standardized scales which can be adapted as well as general approaches to attitude research.)

Wells, William D. (ed.). *Life Style and Psychographics.* Chicago: American Marketing Association, 1974.

7

Going Into the Field

Once the questionnaire has been finalized, the next step in the research process (stage number 6, Figure 3) is the actual collection of the data from the field. Often this requires the use of personal interviewers. This chapter discusses procedures required to select and train interviewers and the actual conduct of a successful interview.

INTERVIEWER SELECTION AND TRAINING

The role of the interviewer is to win the cooperation of the respondent initially and to collect unbiased information. This means that he or she must be an absolutely *neutral* factor in the whole process. Obviously this is easier said than done, because the interviewer must process the information through a filter which contains attitudes, personality traits, etc. The result all too often is that recorded information deviates in significant ways from that actually given by respondents.[1] Republican interviewers, for example, tend to report a higher incidence of Republican political preference than their Democratic counterparts. The dangers of interviewer bias are sufficiently large to require the exercise of great care in selection, training, and compensation.

---

[1] For a thorough review of the problem of interviewer bias, see Harper W. Boyd, Jr. and Ralph Westfall, *Marketing Research: Text and Cases,* 3rd ed. (Homewood, Ill.: Richard D. Irwin, Inc., 1972), ch. 11

Selection of Interviewers

In earlier years it often was believed that one could select an "interviewer type" on the basis of personality and background characteristics. This theory has been largely discredited, however, because experience shows that most people can function successfully as interviewers with proper training and motivation.

What, then, should one look for when selecting an interviewer? There is only one definitive rule of practice — select those whose background, appearance, and temperament are compatible with those in the sample. An interviewer who differs too radically will not be well received. A white person, for instance, rarely can function successfully as an interviewer with inner-city blacks in the United States. It is equally true that a North American will more often than not be viewed with suspicion by those living in the developing countries unless that person is known and accepted.

Keeping in mind that interviewers must be a neutral factor, common sense would suggest that the best interviewers usually are "ordinary people." It probably also goes without saying that they should demonstrate some ability to converse freely without undue introversion. Other than these few considerations, little more can be stated in the way of qualifications.

Training

Training usually takes place in two phases: (1) general instruction in procedures discussed later in the chapter, and (2) supervised field work. In the first stage, the questionnaire is reviewed in detail, and the candidate is introduced to the principles of interviewing. It is wise to introduce supervised practice to make sure that the principles have been grasped which then will be followed by actual supervised field interviewing. The supervisor notes both strengths and weaknesses of the interviewer and reviews these immediately.

Compensation

A commonsense rule of any area of human endeavor is that one "gets what he pays for." It frequently is possible to utilize volunteers in Christian work because of their personal interest in the project. Their "payment" is the satisfaction derived. When it is necessary to make actual financial remuneration, wage rates should be at least equal to the prevailing level for comparable work. Two payment options are available: (1) hourly rate and (2) payment per completed interview.

The hourly rate offers the advantage that interviewers are not unduly hurried to complete a quota during a given period and hence sacrifice quality for quantity. Also, compensation is given for greater than usual travel time. Payment per completed interview, on the other hand, permits tighter budgetary control. It is possible to estimate with precision what the field costs will be.

All things being equal, the author has found that the best results are achieved when an hourly (or daily) rate is used. Generally the quality of performance is better. Moreover, budgetary control will not be a problem if interviewers are well trained and have learned how to schedule their time appropriately.

THE INTERVIEWING PROCESS

There are three important aspects of the interviewing process: (1) *achievement of respondent cooperation;* (2) *conduct of the interview;* and (3) *evaluation of completed work.*

Achievement of Cooperation

It is virtually impossible to approach a home without at least some suspicion incurred on the part of those being contacted. The environment for personal interviewing in North America has been substantially damaged by the ubiquity of salesmen posing as interviewers. Also the growing crime problem leads many to avoid any kind of response to strangers.

Therefore, it is necessary to take definite steps to insure the credibility of the interviewer and to gain the respondent's confidence.

One of the most important aids in credibility is to use the endorsement of respected officials. The objective of one Wheaton Research project was to interview school-age children and their parents on attitudes toward children's television. A simple random sample of homes was chosen from school directories with the approval of local officials. A letter was sent in advance to these homes signed by the author as project director and by the Superintendent of Schools. The purpose of the study was explained, and cooperation was requested. Interviewers then telephoned these homes and requested an interview time. The response was unprecedented in that there were virtually no refusals. In fact, people were awaiting the call. In part this reflected high interest in the subject matter, but there is no question that the letter was an effective door opener.

In the developing countries, the process of achieving endorsements is both essential and demanding. It may be necessary to start with officials at the top of the government and work down stage by stage to the local level. Once this is done, doors open with much less suspicion. In effect, trusted authorities are saying, "It's okay — cooperate with these people because they are our friends." If this step is not taken, there may be no cooperation whatsoever.

Advance notification always is a helpful procedure whenever possible. This may be in the form of a letter or a telephone call. The author recently directed a study in which this step was not possible. The refusal rate was astonishingly high, and it became clear that the resulting sample was not truly representative for this reason alone.

If no advance notification is utilized, the wording of the introduction then carries the entire burden. As a rule, the interviewer states his or her name and briefly states the purpose of the project in general terms so as to avoid biasing the questions which follow. It is important not to be deceptive in this introduction, but it is not necessary to reveal the sponsor and some of the detailed purposes at the outset when that can only serve to contaminate the responses. The amount of time required always should be indicated. It is unfair to ask for a few minutes when the interview, in reality, may take much longer.

The reader is directed to Figure 19 for an example of a well-worded introduction. The name is stated; the general sponsor is identified; and a broad statement of purpose is given. This was a relatively short questionnaire, although it would have been better, in retrospect, to ask for about thirty minutes of their time. The interviewer wore a badge as identification and was free to state that local officials had been notified that this project was legitimate.

Conduct of the Interview

A portion of the interviewer guide prepared for the study of adults in Vancouver appears in Figure 19. It contains a brief but comprehensive review of the elements of effective interviewing. Rather than restate what it says, just a few additional comments are given to highlight some key points.

Jesus walked and lived among the people of His time. Thus, He was enabled to use words, parables, examples which spoke directly to their needs and backgrounds. In this sense, Jesus was using an excellent form of audience research — observation. This survey project has precisely the same objective: a focusing of the Word of God to speak effectively to modern man. The difference, of course, is that the objective calls for reaching millions and hence different methods of research and communication are required.

The survey has always been used by communicators, although the onset of questionnaire and sampling methods is a modern phenomenon. It is basically a tool of inquiry and nothing more. Because the goal is to *understand* other people and to grasp their backgrounds and points of view, all involved in this project must strive for objectivity. Objectivity, in turn, requires that certain rules of interviewing practice be followed. This guide is prepared for that purpose.

SOME FUNDAMENTALS OF
EFFECTIVE INTERVIEWING

1. *Go only to the houses you have been assigned.* Each interviewer will

be given a list of homes which are eligible to be interviewed. You are not free to substitute other homes without approval from the Reachout office. The reason for this is that we have gone to great expense and effort to guarantee that we will have a representative sample of the Greater Vancouver area. Unless we follow this rule, we could easily wind up with a distorted picture.

2. *Use a friendly and neutral introduction to gain cooperation.* We would suggest you use an introduction something like this:

"Hello, I'm _____. I'm part of a group of greater Vancouver residents who are working with "People to People." We are from community groups and churches of all types, and we are taking a survey with thousands all over the city to find out basic community needs and concerns. This will only take a few minutes. May I come in?"

Experiment a bit with this and find out what works for you. Be natural, and be yourself. Display your badge prominently. If there is reluctance, share the introduction letter. Also, we are fully registered with police and other agencies. Occasionally people will check to see.

3. *Do everything you can to complete the interview once you have found someone home.* There often will be some reluctance to go ahead, but a natural, friendly attitude on your part will be a great help. Assure them that all replies are completely anonymous. Call back again at a better time if necessary. Make an appointment right then, and keep it!

4. *Remember your role is to uncover opinion, not to change it.* We want to discover spiritual awareness, interest, and beliefs. Change will occur later as we get into the Reachout program. This is *not* an opportunity for evangelism. If you have an open door for that, call back later on your own.

5. *Conduct the interview in a natural, conversational manner.* Just be yourself.

6. *Ask the questions only as they are worded.* This is very important. Just a slight change of wording can lead to a very different meaning. Therefore, read the question only as it is asked on your questionnaires. If it is not understood, repeat the question just as it is worded. Do not attempt to explain it! If there is no understanding, just leave blank and go on.

7. *Record answers fully as they are given.* Usually all we require is a check mark in the proper place. A few are structured as "open end."

Going Into the Field

Do everything you can to get down the exact words. *Listen carefully!* Try to capture what they say, not what you think they said. So record it fully at the time, and do not attempt to change it later. Memory can play tricks. It is helpful to check these answers over to be sure your handwriting is legible, but adding comments should be done only when you are sure you missed something they actually said.

8. *Follow all directions on the questionnaire.* Question order, for example, CANNOT BE CHANGED. Do it exactly as it appears. There are good reasons for everything that is being done.

9. *Ask every question, no matter how sensitive it appears to be.* Every item of information is important.

10. *Probe where answers are not fully given.* This applies only on the open end questions. Use a neutral probe such as "Can you tell me more?" "Is there anything else?" Be careful not to comment as they comment. It is absolutely wrong to say something like: "Yes, that's a good idea," etc. Only use neutral probes. Anything other than that can change opinion rather than reflect it.

THE SAMPLE

In the community survey, we are attempting to complete 2500 interviews with adults. Your list of homes will have many more than the 13 we wish you to contact. This is because we inevitably will find some who are not at home no matter how many times we try or who just will not cooperate. Therefore, you are free to substitute the next name on the list each time this happens.

Let's assume you have called on a home and no one is home. Try again *one other time* at a different time of day. Much of our work will have to be done in the evening or we will wind up with too many housewives. If a callback produces no response, go to the next name. Do the same if you have a refusal.

We want you to attempt to get about half men and half women in your 13 completed surveys. Do everything you can to bring this about, recognizing that women sometimes are more willing to cooperate than men. Calling as a couple, however, really reduces this reluctance. *Never* interview both husband and wife in a given home. Interview just one person per home.

CONDUCTING THE INTERVIEW

Try to get in the home. Sometimes this is difficult, but most people invite you in. Then, ask the name of the person you are interviewing. Almost always this should be the man or woman of the house only. Find a comfortable location where you can be uninterrupted if possible. If the television is blaring or kids are making a ruckus, suggest another location. Usually the best bet is to suggest the kitchen or dining room table in that case.

Try to get your respondent (either male or female) alone. If others are there, point out that you are trying to get individual responses. Be tactful about this. If you are calling as husband and wife, one partner quickly can divert the distractors.

Only one person should conduct the interview. The wife may want to carry the ball most of the time, although this is up to you. The other partner sits quietly and does not get involved.

Figure 19. A Guide for Interviewers:
Vancouver Reachout Survey

It always is best to conduct an interview in a natural, conversational manner. But, no changes whatsoever are permitted in question wording unless this has been stated in training as being allowable in specific instances. If wording varies from one interviewer to another, then the results are invalidated.

Interviewers also should be aware that changes in voice intonation and gestures can be a source of bias. What would happen, for example, if voice stress were placed on the italicized words in this question?

In the presidential election held last week, did you vote for the *socialist candidate* or the Christian democratic candidate?

In the presidential election held last week, did you vote for the socialist candidate or the *Christian democratic* candidate?

The stress on the party name may lead the respondent to state that party regardless of actual voting behavior. Similar results can be achieved through indiscreet nods and other forms of gesture which serve to encourage one answer over another.

The interviewing guide in Figure 19 also stresses the importance of privacy during the interview itself. This may be nothing more than an ideal when research is undertaken in the developing countries. The presence of an interviewer often will attract a crowd, and it may be completely impossible to get the respondent alone. Furthermore, everyone will have his say, and the results may be more of a group consensus than anything else. Frankly, this may be unavoidable, and it is best to design the project in full awareness that this can happen. All one can do is strive for privacy but accept the circumstance as they arise.

Another problem is to gain access to the desired respondent. This can be particularly troublesome when the respondent is a woman. In some Muslim countries, women are not who will reply. Perhaps the growing trend toward sexual equality worldwide, especially in the major cities, will alleviate this dilemma somewhat. But it can be totally beyond solution. Cultural norms do not readily bend to the researcher's wishes.

Evaluation of Completed Work

There are several ways in which interview work can be unsatisfactory: (1) outright falsification; (2) selective questioning (some but not all questions are asked); (3) choice of wrong respondent; and (4) interview of a group rather than specified individuals (assuming there is cultural access to the individual).

The author once used a field force of thirty interviewers and was surprised when his assistant identified a serious error on the questionnaires turned in by the field supervisor. The interviewers were unaware that all respondents had recently purchased a particular brand of automobile. An introductory question, used simply as an icebreaker, asked which make of automobile was owned by the family. This woman interviewer reported quite a variety of answers, and it was clear that something was wrong. Upon confrontation, she admitted that all questionnaires had been filled out in her home and thereby totally falsified. Unfortunately, this is not uncommon.

In this instance a filter question detected falsification. At other times, it will be necessary to undertake spot checks with some respondents to verify that they indeed were interviewed. A bit of probing also can verify whether or not correct procedures were followed.

Another aspect of the evaluation phase is to check the cost per completed interview. Some may be wasting time, and this will show up in a cost level which deviates from the norm.

A third consideration is success in following instructions. This is best evaluated by a review of the questionnaires as they are turned in. One should always be certain that all questions were asked and that complete answers are recorded.

Finally, it is worthwhile to analyze the number of refusals generated by each interviewer. An interviewer with an abnormally high level may be utilizing an introduction which is failing to achieve cooperation. This can be corrected easily by remedial training.

To Sum Up

Interviewing is more of an art than a science, yet good interviewing skills can be learned. A well-chosen sample and carefully pretested questionnaire will all be for naught if the interviewer deviates from absolute neutrality and introduces bias. The rules of practice discussed in this chapter will help in minimizing bias. Careful training, adequate compensation, and analytical supervision also will be of help.

For Further Reading

Backstrom, Charles H. and Hursh, Gerald D. *Survey Research.* Evanston, Ill.: Northwestern University Press, 1963, ch. 5.

Boyd, Harper W., Jr. and Westfall, Ralph. *Marketing Research: Text and Cases,* 3rd ed. Homewood, Ill.: Richard D. Irwin, Inc., 1972, ch. 11.

Ferber, Robert (ed.). *Handbook of Marketing Research.* New York: McGraw-Hill Book Company, 1974. Part B, chs. 5-8.

Gorden, Raymond L. *Interviewing: Strategy, Techniques, and Tactics.* Homewood, Ill.: The Dorsey Press, 1969.

8

Data Tabulation, Analysis, and Reporting

We now have reached the last methodological stage of the research process in Figure 3 — tabulation, analysis, and reporting of the data. Tabulation and analysis procedures can be quite technical, but the discussion here is introductory. Once again, the reader interested in greater depth should consult the sources listed at the end of the chapter.

TABULATION

There are two preliminary steps prior to actual tabulation: (1) *editing* and (2) *coding*. Then tabulation can be done by hand, by manual punch card, or by machine.

Editing

The editing step is undertaken to insure that the questionnaire has been adequately completed according to instructions. The interviewer does the initial editing, but it also is necessary usually to perform a more detailed edit in the office.

Here is a useful check list to follow:

1. Are all questions answered? If not, the questionnaire may be discarded depending upon the frequency of omissions. An occasional omission may be of little consequence.

2. Is the handwriting legible? If not, it may be necessary to rewrite the answers so that they can be read by the keypuncher or tabulator.

3. Are patterns of response consistent? It often is wise to insert questions as a check on interviewer and respondent honesty. This assumes some prior knowledge of respondents. Also, it is a sound practice to use more than one measure for important objectives. Where there is evidence of outright dishonesty or consistent response contradiction, the questionnaire should be discarded.

Coding

It always is desirable to use a precoded questionnaire, and the procedures for that purpose were discussed in chapter 5. Sometimes this is not done, and there may be open-end questions on a precoded instrument which will require additional coding. Coding is a step whereby numbers are assigned to answers so they may be entered on a mechanical tabulation card.

When open-end questions are utilized, the usual policy is to read perhaps 25 percent of the incoming questionnaires to delineate the categories of response given. Each of these then is assigned a number for keypunching. The coding step, then, is a matter of using judgment to determine the appropriate response category for each question.

At times no attempt will be made to tabulate open-end questions. Rather, they are analyzed qualitatively by reading each one and sensing the impact of what is said. It is helpful to abstract actual verbatim comments and to utilize them in that form in the final report.

Tabulation.

The ideal tabulation method, of course, is to keypunch the coded questionnaires and to utilize a computer both for actual counting and for statistical analysis. Computers are not always readily available, however. Furthermore, not all computers will be available with the statistical programs necessary for this type of processing. Therefore, it often is necessary to ship the completed questionnaires to a central location where such facilities are available. This is far from ideal because of the time required.

Moreover, questionnaires can be lost in transit. Only about 60 percent of the completed questionnaires from the survey of Christians in Brazil ever arrived at Wheaton for processing. There are records that they were shipped, but a large number have been lost in transit. Fortunately, an adequate sample was achieved, but this still represents a tragic loss.

If a computer is not available, the Indecks method discussed in chapter 5 is the next best option. The reader will recall that this approach is similar to keypunching in that it utilizes a card on which answers are mechanically punched. All tabulation is done by hand, however.

Hand tabulation is possible only if there is a very small sample and/or a short questionnaire. It is done by marking tally sheets. The difficulty enters when it is necessary to cross-tabulate or segregate answers into subgroups by age, income, and so on. This becomes totally unwieldy with hand tabulation. Generally, hand tabulation should be avoided unless the Indecks system is used.

DATA ANALYSIS AND INTERPRETATION

The researcher must specify the requirements for tabulation and cross-tabulation. Then data are analyzed through use of statistical methods and through the use of logic. Each of these steps is discussed in turn.

Straight Tabulation of Data

The starting point is a frequency count of the answers given by the entire sample to each question. Then percentages are computed. It is helpful to transfer both the frequency counts and the percentages directly onto a copy of the questionnaire itself so that responses can be grasped at a glance. I have discovered, along the way, that it usually is necessary to combine the two extreme response categories on each end of an agree/disagree scale into one for purposes of frequency counts. As was mentioned earlier, many people will not utilize the extreme scale positions, and the frequencies of reply thus will be unduly small.

Cross-tabulation

Straight tabulations are helpful in providing a general picture, but the underlying dynamics are obscured. One has no way to segregate the responses in one subgroup from those in another. This is the purpose of cross-tabulation.

The usual starting point is to cross-classify answers by demographic characteristics, especially age, sex, and socioeconomic status. Variations may provide clues to differences in receptivity between audience subgroups and the best ways to reach them.

It also is helpful to designate the questions which are the key measures of felt need for change in life. Often these are questions centering on meaning and purpose. In order to differentiate those who are seeking from those who are not, there is great value in cross-tabulation by these variables. The result is a clear picture of all responses given by seekers and those given by the nonseekers, and this too can give great insight into strategy.

Figure 20 provides an example of a cross-classification table in which readership of four Christian magazines is analyzed by age. For purposes of simplicity, only two age categories are used.

| MAGAZINES | AGE CATEGORY | | | | | |
| | UNDER 35 | | 35 AND OVER | | TOTAL | |
	No.	%	No.	%	No.	%
A	60	30.0%	280	35.0%	340	34.0%
B	40	20.0	170	21.3	210	21.0
C	30	15.0	40	5.0	70	7.0
D	70	35.0	310	38.7	380	38.0
TOTAL	200	100.0%	800	100.0%	1000	100.0%

Figure 20. Christian Magazine Readership Cross-Classified by Age

Notice, first of all, that the cross-classification variable is placed across the top of the table. The percentages are computed downward by columns — i.e., the column total is utilized as the percentage base. This is the usual procedure in cross-classification analysis. The row totals are nothing more than the straight tabulation of readership for each magazine.

Now, what does this table tell us? First, there are some readership differences between age groups. Younger respondents (those under 35), in particular, seem to prefer magazine C. Yet the differences are not large. There is an obvious need for further analysis, and the next step is to evaluate these differences statistically.

Statistical Analysis

Analysis of Confidence Intervals. Let's return, for a moment, to the straight tabulation using the example in Figure 20. Here the data tell us that 34 percent read magazine A, 21 percent read magazine B, 7 percent read magazine C, and 38 percent read magazine D. How representative is this of the total target population (or universe to use the statistician's term)?

The reader will recall the discussion of confidence intervals in chapter 4. There always is a range of error which must be taken into consideration when generalizing from sample data to the population, and this can be measured if random sampling has been used. Assuming our sample was chosen at random, we now can refer to the table in Figure 7 to evaluate the width of our confidence interval. Here we discover that we can be 95 percent confident that the true figure "out there" is somewhere in the interval of our sample statistic ± 3 percent. Therefore, the actual readership of magazine A is somewhere between 31 and 37 percent.

Data interpretation always must take confidence intervals into account. This is especially true if this interval is quite wide, in which case greater caution must be taken in attributing precision to the answers. The books referenced at the end of the chapter are helpful in explaining the computation and interpretation of

135

confidence intervals. Most readers, of course, need not be concerned with these mechanical considerations.

Significance of Differences Between Subgroups. We observed that the differences in readership between the four magazines in Figure 20 are not large. In fact, it is possible that these reflect only *chance variations.* If so, then the differences themselves are of no managerial significance. Chance always is a possibility when one is working with data drawn from samples.

Fortunately, it is possible to measure statistically whether or not such differences are due simply to chance. There is a whole family of statistical methods which can be utilized, and each is applicable under precisely stated conditions. Most readers will not be interested in these technical details, and those who are will find help in the sources listed at the end of the chapter.

There is one statistical method which is widely used to assess the meaning of differences of this type and which is not beyond the grasp of the reader. In words, it is referred to as *chi square analysis,* and usually it is depicted in statistical symbols as follows: x^2 The formula for this statistic is given below, and the reader is urged to put down that inevitible defense mechanism rearing its ugly head from the days of high school algebra. Remember that mathematical notation is merely shorthand for what can be said in words. So, here goes:

$$x^2 = \sum \frac{(O-E)^2}{E}$$

where,

$\sum =$ sum of

$O =$ the actual answer given by members of the subgroup (say, an age group)

$E =$ the answer one would expect members of the subgroup to give if there were no differences from one subgroup to another.

Put in words, it will be necessary to compare the actual observed value (O) in each cell of a table against that value which would be expected (E) if there were no differences from one subgroup to the next. The 60 people in Figure 20 under the age of 35 who read magazine A thus would be noted as the observed value for that cell of the table and so on. The expected value must be computed, however.

Now, how does one compute the expected value? Looking again at Figure 20, one would expect that 34 percent of those in each age group would read magazine A if there were no differences between the two groups. The 34 percent figure appears as the total at the end of the first row. And 21 percent would read magazine B and so on. The expected readership of magazine A by those under 35, then, would be 68, which is 34 percent of 200 (200 is the total number of males in the sample who are under 35). An identical computation is made for each cell in the table, and the results of this simple computation appear in Figure 21. Observed values are designated by O and expected values by E.

Magazines	AGE CATEGORY				
	Under 35		35 and over		Total
	O	E	O	E	
Total					
A	60	68	280	272	340
B	40	42	170	168	210
C	30	14	40	56	70
D	70	76	310	304	380

Figure 21. A Comparison of Observed and Expected Readership of Four Christian Magazines Cross-Classified by Age

Now we have the basis to compute x^2. First take the difference between the observed and the expected value for the first cell in the table (readership of magazine A by those under 35). This gives a value of 8. Now, according to the formula, that value should be squared (the number 8 multiplied by itself) and divided by the expected value 68. This is 64 divided by 68 which, in turn, equals .94. That figure is jotted down, and an identical computation is made for all remaining cells in the table. Then all of these figures are summed into one total, and that gives us the computed value of x^2. In this example, $x^2 =$ 24.799.

We now have to make one more simple computation and we then are ready to determine if these differences in readership are real or merely are the result of chance variations. We count the number of rows in the table and subtract 1 from that figure (4 - 1 = 3). We do the same for the number of columns, not counting the total as a column (2 - 1 = 1). Now we multiply these two figures and this gives what the statistician has labeled the number of *degrees of freedom.* The formula for degrees of freedom is (r - 1) (c - 1), where "r" is the number of rows and "c" the number of columns. The number of degrees of freedom in Figure 20, then, is 3 (3 x 1).

Now we are ready to consult the x^2 table, a portion of which is reproduced in Figure 22. It gives what is known as the *critical value* for each degree of freedom. If our computed chi square value exceeds that figure, there is less than a 5 percent chance that differences as large as those observed in the data are due to chance. We then can safely assume in the example used here that there is a real difference in magazine preference and readership from one age group to the next. Notice that the critical value for 3 degrees of freedom is 7.815, whereas our computed value is 24.799. It is apparent that these differences may not be explained away by chance. To use the statistician's terms, we may conclude that the differences are *statistically significant* (not due to chance).

Data Tabulation, Analysis, and Reporting

Degrees of Freedom	Critical Value
1	3.841
2	5.991
3	7.815
4	9.488
5	11.07
6	12.59
7	14.07
8	15.51
9	16.92
10	18.31
11	19.68
12	21.03
13	22.36
14	23.68
15	25.00
16	26.30
17	27.59
18	28.87
19	30.14
20	31.41

Figure 22. A Portion of the χ^2 Table Showing the Critical Values at the 95% Confidence Level for Degrees of Freedom Ranging From 1-20.[1]

It is possible that one would have thousands of cross-tabulation tables in a large-scale computer analysis. The first step is to go through and assess which, if any, are statistically significant as we have done here. If this is not possible, focus only on those tables in which the differences obviously are so large that they could not be due to chance.

Logical Interpretation

Now that chance has been rejected as the explanation, let's refer back to Figure 20 to detect the source of the variations. The differences in readership between magazines A, B, and D by members of these two age groups are not great. The largest

---

[1]Source: This table was adapted from *Biometrika*, Vol. 32 (1941-42) pp. 188—89 by special permission.

difference is 10 percent with magazine C. It is favored by readers under age 35 more than it is by their older counterparts.

This is a good illustration of the fact that statistical significance (i.e., rejection of chance) does not necessarily imply *managerial significance*. In other words, one could legitimately conclude that readership differences of this magnitude do not warrant changes in strategy. Usually the author follows the general rule that responses in any given subgroup must deviate from those given by the total sample by at least 10 percent before serious consideration is given to changes in strategy. Obviously there will be instances in which such a rule should be modified, but it is an acceptable general guideline.

Here are some other considerations which might prove to be of help:

1. Do not attempt to produce "startling results." Often the outcome will be nothing more than confirmation of the expected. There is no reason to expect that research always will uncover something that is dramatically new.

2. Do not overemphasize favorable evidence. Always check to see that all evidence is reported. Sometimes there will be hesitance to stress the negative, especially if it will place a client in a bad light.

3. Do not be dazzled by complexity. There are some researchers who use statistical terms as a "snow job." The uninitiated reader may conclude that data are valid for this reason alone, when quite the opposite may, in fact, be the case. Simplicity and clarity are the hallmarks of the sensitive, managerially oriented researcher.

4. Do not place too much faith in averages. These are only a measure of central tendency, and the great range of underlying response can be obscured.

5. Do not mistake respondent opinion for fact. What the person thinks is never an infallible indication of the true situation. This, of course, is not to say that attitudes and opinions are of no value in research. It merely places this kind of information in perspective.

The Report

The report itself often is the key to acceptance or rejection of the findings and recommendations. Always bear in mind that the report must be written from the perspective of those who are responsible for implementing the recommendations. The probability is that they have relatively little interest in technical detail. Complex terminology, tables, and charts have little place in reports where the goal is to motivate and facilitate managerial action.

It is suggested that the report be organized in the following manner: (1) *executive summary;* (2) *introduction and statement of problem;* (3) *methodology;* (4) *data analysis;* (5) *recommendations;* and (6) *appendices.*

Executive Summary

A two- to four-page summary is the single most important part of the report, and often it is the only section that an action-oriented executive will read. He or she will want to know, in a nutshell, what the purpose of the study was, what the findings were, and the implications for action. If this cannot be said in a few pages, rewrite the summary.

It has been said that Winston Churchill required a leading military aide to describe the position of the entire Atlantic fleet during World War II on one side of one sheet of paper. When the aide objected that it was impossible, Churchill did not relent. And, in the process, the impossible became possible!

Introduction

The introduction is the first section in the body of the report itself. It also should be brief — usually less than one page. The sole purpose is to state the goals of the project in specific terms, focusing particularly on the nature of the problem to be investigated.

Methodology

The methodological section should describe the steps

141

taken in sampling, questionnaire design, data analysis, and other technical considerations. This should be written in laymen's terms with the emphasis on the general rather than the specific. If it is felt that details are required, place them in a technical appendix which can be consulted by the interested reader.

Data Analysis

This section usually is organized around the major research objectives. Straight tabulations are presented first in graphic terms whenever possible. This can be done in the form of a bar graph (Figure 23), a pie chart (Figure 24), or a line graph (Figure 25). The purpose is to guarantee that the main points are readily grasped. Complex tables generally have no place in the body of the report. Most will not take the time to study them, and they may serve only to confuse rather than to edify. When additional detail is needed, use the appendices for this purpose.

I believe there is a God — **57.0%**

Jesus was God — **33.7**%

God is of central importance — **23.7**%

The Bible is God's revealed word — **29.9**%

Religion is important for man — **43.1**%

Only one religion leads to God — **12.6**%

Right or wrong is only one man's opinion — **42.4**%

God is satisfied if a person lives the best life he can — **44.2**%

I would have to be called a skeptic or agnostic — **18.1**%

Education has most of the answers for moral and social problems — **18.2**%

142

I try to carry religion over into other activities of life 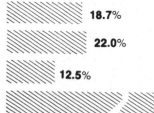 **18.7%**

I have read the Bible at least once in the past month **22.0%**

I have had some experiences with the occult **12.5%**

Most of the world's problems are caused by man himself **75%**

Figure 23. An Example of a Bar Graph
Spiritual Awareness and Beliefs*

*Percentages who replied "strongly agree" or "agree"

Religious Classification of Respondents

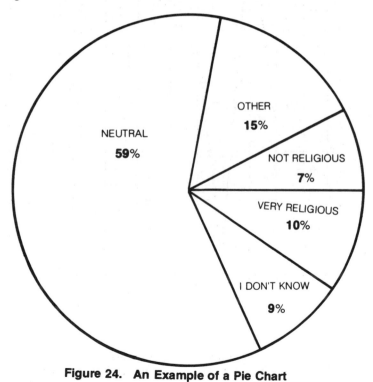

NEUTRAL
59%

OTHER
15%

NOT RELIGIOUS
7%

VERY RELIGIOUS
10%

I DON'T KNOW
9%

Figure 24. An Example of a Pie Chart

143

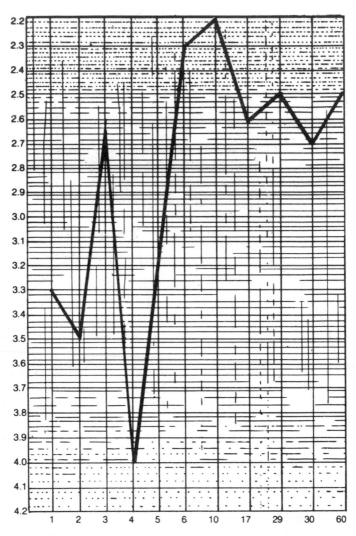

Figure 25. A Line Graph
Ratings of Radio Spots (spots are designated by number):

Data Tabulation, Analysis, and Reporting

Cross-classification data should follow presentation and discussion of the straight tabulations. This quickly can become detailed and voluminous, especially when many of these cross tabulations have managerial significance. Usually the best approach is to avoid tables and graphs and describe the significant tabulations in narrative form.

The discussion should, of course, focus on interpretation and conclusions. Usually the recommendations for action will be restated later, but the reader must be assisted in arriving at correct conclusions. At times the analyst will be forced to present several alternative explanations for data patterns and leave the final conclusion for the reader, but the discussion must at least present the competing options.

Recommendations

The author long has been of the conviction that the researcher is obligated to state conclusions and recommendations for action. Others feel that the researcher should only be a reporter. The latter point of view, however, takes away the benefit of a certain degree of objectivity and expertise which a qualified outsider will possess. Granted, the researcher rarely will have a full grasp of all factors which affect decisions, but useful insights still may be contributed.

Recommendations always must be stated as representing the opinion of the researcher. If presented as the final word on the subject then further analysis and discussion is impossible. Dogmatic wording must be avoided in this section *at all costs*.

Appendices

At the Wheaton Graduate School we make it a practice to include at least one appendix to every report. The first appendix always will be a copy of the questionnaire which also contains the frequencies and percentages of response for each answer, printed right on the questionnaire itself. This enables the reader to grasp the entire pattern of answers, and it also is a real space saver in the presentation itself. Other appendices can be utilized to present additional backup detail and data. Do not use this section as a "dumping ground," however, because most readers avoid the appendices altogether.

The Oral Report

It always is advantageous to give an oral presentation to accompany the written report. Preferably it will precede the writeup. Good oral presentation calls for ample use of visual aids. Overhead transparencies, flip charts, and other types of graphic aids should be prepared for each major piece of data presented. Words alone cannot suffice. Keep the presentation logical and nontechnical, realizing again that the greatest concern of the audience will be with the conclusions and the recommendations.

Concluding Comments

The essence of successful reporting may be stated succinctly: keep it short, simple, and practical. This should not be interpreted as a call for a moratorium on discussion of complex issues. Rather, it underscores the fact that research findings must be communicated if they are to be used.

I have a longstanding practice used when analyzing research reports prepared by others. If the report contains too many tables and technical details, it is returned when possible with a note stating, "Please translate into English." This is just my way of saying, "I expect you to write this so that I can understand it without taking an undue amount of time."

To Sum Up

The first step after field work is completed is to edit and code the data, assuming that the questionnaire has not been precoded. Ideally, there then will be access to a computer. If not, recourse must be made to some form of manual tabulation.

The starting point in the analysis stage is to tabulate the response to all questions and compute a percentage. Then data should be cross classified into appropriate subgroups. Demographic cross classification (i.e., education, social status, and age) is a standard practice. The goal here is to isolate whether or not there are response differences within subgroups of the sample. When such differences are observed, these may only reflect chance variations. Therefore, these data must be analyzed statistically to reject chance as the explanation, and one procedure for this purpose, chi square analysis, was discussed. Then the emphasis shifts to a managerial analysis where the key question always is, "What does this mean for strategy?"

It was stressed that the final report is a crucial factor in the acceptance or rejection of findings by users. It always must be written with the audience in mind, in full recognition that most are interested in the implications, not in technical detail.

For Further Reading

Backstrom, Charles H. and Hursh, Gerald D. *Survey Research.* Evanston, Ill.: Northwestern University Press, 1963, ch. 6 (data processing).

Boyd, Harper W., Jr. and Westfall, Ralph. *Marketing Research: Text and Cases.* Homewood, Ill.: Richard D. Irwin, Inc., 1972, chs. 12 (data analysis) and 13 (reporting).

Churchill, Gilbert A., Jr. *Marketing Research: Methodological Foundations.* Hinsdale, Ill.: The Dryden Press, 1976, chs. 11-15 (excellent general source on statistical analysis) and 16 (the report).

Emory, C. William, *Business Research Methods.* Homewood, Ill.: Richard D. Irwin, Inc., 1976, chs. 12 (tabulation), 13 (statistical analysis), and 14 (reports).

9

Putting the Project Together

We now have covered the first seven stages of the research process in Figure 3. Before proceeding to the last step, phasing research into strategy, it will be helpful to pause and discuss how an actual field survey was conceived, designed, and implemented. The project to be reviewed in this chapter is a survey of high school students undertaken in Quito, Ecuador for purposes of developing a multiple-media evangelistic outreach. While no survey ever can be considered ideal, this will provide a good example of how a spiritual status analysis is done.

THE ECUADORIAN HIGH SCHOOL STUDENT

By way of background, the Wheaton Graduate School initiated a field masters program in Communications in Ecuador in 1974. Encompassing missionaries from HCJB and the Gospel Missionary Union, this program is the first phase in a long-term strategy designed to provide training for national leaders in South American countries. These missionaries now are training future Latin American leaders.

Most of the course work encompassed actual field experience. It was agreed by all who were involved that a strategy must be developed to reach the youth if Christianity ever is to make an impact in Ecuador. The survey discussed in this chapter was designed as part of the requirements for a course in survey research. It actually was completed in the spring of 1975.

Then a complete communication strategy was designed and presented to key leaders in the summer of that year as part of further coursework. As of this writing, final details of implementation still are under consideration.

The Situation in Quito

Evangelical Christians make up 1 percent of the population of Ecuador. This figure is only 0.6 percent in the capital city of Quito, a metropolitan area of over 600,000. The situation is even more critical among the youth. One out of every ten people in Quito is in high school, and not more than 300 are involved in some type of church youth group. No one has ever mounted a strategy to reach this important segment, in spite of the large concentration of missionaries in the city. Youth assume special importance when it is realized that most go on to colleges and universities which are dominated by communist emphasis.

In Quito itself, there are only forty-eight evangelical meeting places, and it is apparent that the church is making little impact on the population as a whole. While there have been a number of well-attended evangelistic campaigns, they have not resulted in church growth. Furthermore, many churches are without a pastor, and few can afford the luxury of a full-time paid leader. Not surprisingly, pastors are clamoring for training in how to increase their effectiveness.

Initial Steps in Survey Planning

The initial design for a spiritual analysis of Quito youth was essentially complete by January, 1975. As of April, however, no actual steps had yet been taken toward implementation. Part of the delay was due to fear that governmental clearance would not be given to approach the high schools.

Early in April a committee of four agreed upon the following survey objective:

> To study the habits, interests, and attitudes of Quito high school juniors and seniors in order to plan a multiple media approach in

Putting the Project Together

reaching these young people with the Gospel.

The questionnaire was finalized by April 25, and an appointment was scheduled with the General Director of the Ministry of Education. A committee consisting of two missionaries and one national leader met with the General Director who suggested minor changes in several questions. Permission then was granted to enter at least six schools, and he sent a letter of endorsement to each school.

The questionnaire then was corrected, pretested, and printed. National leaders were involved in the first two phases here, and the pretest verified that the instrument communicated as intended. Contacts then were made with the different schools. Excellent cooperation was achieved from most, and the survey was begun in classrooms on May 20.

The Questionnaire

The questionnaire used appears in Figure 26. The process of backward translation causes loss of some of the nuances of the Spanish language, but it provides a good indication of the construction of specific questions. The percentages of response given also are included.

1. Name of school _____

2. Course specialization _____

3. Do you intend to continue studies in college?

    1. 84.5 Yes   2. 3.7 No   3. 10.3 I don't know

4. What kind of work would you like to do when you finish your studies?

_____

5. What activity occupied the major part of your time yesterday afternoon?

    1.   1.7 movies   5.   3.6 practicing music
    2.   5.7 sports   6.   6.8 reading
    3.   4.4 TV   7. 27.4 studying

How Can I Get Them to Listen?

4. 17.4 chatting with friends   8. 15.2 other (specify)
                                  17.8 — no response

6. What activity occupied the major part of your time last night?
   1.   1.4 sports   6.   0.4 a discotheque
   2.   0.4 movies   7. 25.3 studying
   3. 22.2 TV   8. 14.3 reading
   4. 11.4 chatting with friends   9. 12.3 other (specify)
   5.   0.6 a party   11.7 — no response

7. How many hours did you watch TV yesterday?
   1. 31.6 didn't watch TV   5. 3.4 more than three hours
   2. 28.4 less than one hour   6. 1.3 more than four hours
   3. 24.3 more than one hour   7. 0.3 more than five hours
   4.   9.4 more than two hours   8. 0.3 six hours or more
                                      1.2 — no response

8. What is your favorite TV program? _____

   _____

9. How many hours did you listen to the radio yesterday?
   1. 22.3 didn't listen   5. 7.0 more than three hours
   2. 27.2 less than one hour   6. 4.9 more than four hours
   3. 16.5 more than one hour   7. 2.5 more than five hours
   4. 11.1 more than two hours   8. 5.4 six hours or more
                                      3.1 — no response

10. To which radio station do you listen the most? _____

11. What is the most convenient hour to listen? _____

12. What kind of music do you like the most?

   1. 40.4 classical   5. 28.6 foreign popular
   2. 22.3 folkloric   6. 33.2 Latin American rock
   3. 24.8 Ecuadorian   7. 47.7 foreign rock
   4. 29.0 Latin American   8.   8.9 other (specify)

13. How many records did you buy last month?_____ Cassettes?_____

14. What was the best record that you have bought in the last six months?

   _____

Putting the Project Together

15. What was the best theatrical performance you have seen in the last six months? _____

_____

16. What was the best movie that you saw in the last six months? _____

_____

17. How many movies have you seen in the last six months? _____

18. What is the best magazine you read in the last six months? _____

_____

19. How many magazines did you buy in the last six months? _____

20. In your opinion what section of the newspaper do you read the most or most often?

    1. 37.6 national and local news
    2. 18.9 movie notices
    3. 39.0 international news
    4. 9.5 social news
    5. 39.1 comic section
    6. 57.9 sports
    7. 17.4 cultural news
    8. 4.1 classified ads
    9. 9.8 editorials
    10. 3.5 other _____

21. What was the best book you read in the last six months outside of the books you had to read for regular class work?_____

_____

22. What world political leader do you admire the most? _____

_____

23. Where do you classify yourself in the area of religion?

    1. 6.8 not religious
    2. 9.7 very religious
    3. 59.2 neutral
    4. 9.4 other (specify) _____
    5. 12.3 I don't know

24. Of what religious faith are you? _____

25. Do you have a Bible at home? ____ Yes ____ No

How Can I Get Them to Listen?

26. How often have you attended a religious service in the last year?

   1. 11.6 never
   2. 31.7 3 or 4 times a year
   3. 18.6 2 or 3 times a month
   4. 15.9 almost every week
   5. 17.9 one time a week
   6. 2.8 more than once a week

27. Please mark an "X" that best indicates your position in regard to each statement.

	IN FAVOR OF	UNDECIDED	NOT IN FAVOR OF
1. I'd like to know more about birth control.	79.1	12.1	7.0
2. I'd like to learn more about other religions.	55.7	23.2	18.5
3. At times I feel lonely.	47.6	19.6	29.3
4. Nutrition or bodily nourishment isn't important to me.	21.9	18.3	56.3
5. I'm afraid of dying.	19.3	25.3	53.1
6. I'm concerned about what others think of me.	32.6	21.6	43.4
7. I'd like to know about the universe in which I live.	85.9	8.1	4.3
8. I'd like to express my opinions more openly.	80.4	11.6	5.3
9. I don't like drastic changes in my life.	46.2	22.3	28.3
10. I'm afraid that perhaps I might not marry.	7.1	16.9	73.9

28. Respond according to your belief:

	AGREE	UNDECIDED	DISAGREE
1. I believe that God exists.	79.4	13.9	5.4
2. God is very important in my life.	60.6	23.0	14.1
3. Jesus was God incarnate.	44.8	33.2	18.8
4. Jesus taught the way in which I ought to live.	53.0	26.3	18.2
5. In this day and age, it's very important for mankind to be religious.	22.8	27.7	47.1

29. Here you find a list of personal problems which often confront students in Ecuador. Please indicate for each problem whether it is a great problem, only a preoccupation, or no problem at all.

154

Putting the Project Together

	A GREAT PROB-LEM FOR ME	ONLY A PRE-OCCUPATION	NO PROBLEM AT ALL
1. I don't want to serve in the military.	12.9	32.5	50.3
2. I'm afraid of failing my grade in school.	36.9	42.5	19.5
3. I'm afraid of a political crisis in Ecuador.	26.3	46.8	24.4
4. I don't have sufficient money.	12.6	41.4	33.8
5. I don't get along with my parents.	35.0	18.8	42.8
6. I don't know what kind of work I'll find or get to do in the future.	23.8	43.9	28.3
7. I'm concerned about finding the right person to marry.	18.7	41.7	36.5
8. I have problems regarding sex.	10.8	41.4	45.5
9. I don't have any reason for living.	21.0	15.1	59.2
10. I'm afraid I won't find the kind of work I really like.	20.0	44.5	32.4
11. I don't have sincere friends.	25.2	27.6	43.5
12. I'm not satisfied with my social life.	17.0	35.1	45.3
13. I'm concerned about my family life.	33.8	31.1	32.8
14. I get angry very easily.	36.4	28.5	32.5

30. Mark the appropriate answer which is closest to your oppinion.

	YES	NO	I DON'T KNOW
1. I have more personality than my friends.	30.8	4.5	62.8
2. Often my friends come to me for advice.	60.3	27.5	10.2
3. I think it's important to learn other languages.	89.8	5.0	3.6
4. Couples ought to have sexual relations before marrying.	36.4	35.6	25.3

155

5. I almost always obey my parents
   when I'm home.   74.5   12.5   11.5
6. At times I have drunk alcoholic
   beverages   70.3   27.6   1.2
7. I've had some supernatural
   experiences.   23.5   65.8   9.4
8. I believe that someone can put
   a "hex" on me.   9.2   69.8   17.4
9. My brothers and sisters are
   important to me.   87.6   4.8   5.8
10. Abortion is bad.   38.1   35.7   24.5
11. I like the horoscope.   43.4   40.4   14.3
12. I want to have children when
    I marry.   89.0   3.4   6.7

31. What is your opinion of the following activities? A student (a) can; (b) ought
    not to; or (c) I am not sure:

	CAN	OUGHT NOT TO	I'M NOT SURE
1. Smoke	56.1	34.6	8.0
2. Go to nightclubs	20.7	61.5	15.6
3. Use drugs including marijuana	4.6	87.5	6.1
4. Change religion	57.2	19.2	22.2
5. Read pornographic literature	35.2	45.7	16.3
6. Go to the movies	95.6	1.4	1.4
7. Participate in protests, etc.	63.0	20.9	13.8
8. Be a homosexual	5.4	86.2	6.2
9. Sell or peddle drugs	2.3	93.2	3.2
10. Cheat or copy during an examination	26.6	54.6	17.3
11. Participate in a strike in high school	57.9	24.4	15.5
12. Consult a medium	27.0	48.0	23.5

32. To whom would you go first of all to talk about a personal problem?

1. 9.9 father   6. 1.9 priest
2. 19.7 mother   7. 1.7 relative
3. 8.1 brother/sister   8. 3.5 other _____
4. 25.0 friend   9. 8.3 no one
5. 0.6 teacher

33. Age _____

34. Sex   1. 66.1 masculine   2. 32.3 feminine

156

35. How many brothers and sisters do you have? _____

36. Do you have TV in your house?   1. 94.7 Yes   2. 4.0 No

37. Do you have a telephone at home?   1. 90.5 Yes   2. 7.9 No

38. What profession or work does your father do? _____.

39. How long have you lived in Quito?

   1. 69.2 all my life   5. 1.7 two years
   2. 14.7 more than ten years   6. 0.3 one year
   3. 8.5 more than five years   7. 0.8 less than one year
   4. 3.1 more than three years

40. With whom or where do you live?

   1. 89.4 with my parents   4. 1.2 with a family
   2. 4.3 with my relatives   5. 1.2 in a room
   3. 0.5 in a student boarding 6. 1.7 other _____
      house

Figure 26. The Questionnaire Used to Measure Spiritual Status of High School Students in Quito, Equador (percentages of response are not included)

Notice that the funneling technique was employed. Initial questions were quite general and nonthreatening. The questions then flowed into media exposure, a subject which also is neutral. The more sensitive issues appear later, and spiritual awareness is in the concluding section.

All questions were constructed in full awareness of the cultural characteristic that vulnerability is a weakness. It was decided that frequent use of nonstructured open-end questions would force the student into thinking for himself rather than giving the expected answer. For this reason the questionnaire was not precoded.

Questions 27 and 28 are a mixture of life style, spiritual awareness, and spiritual attitude. Question 29 focuses specifically on felt needs, and question 30 then returns to general life style questions with an altered format. Question 31 provides an

157

interesting index of acceptable versus nonacceptable behavior. Finally, question 32 reveals those who have the greatest influence on the student's life. The remainder of the stimuli are confined to demographic characteristics.

The Sample

An attempt was made to choose six schools which represent a good cross section of all high schools in Quito. This was a purposive, nonrandom sample. Practical considerations prevented the development of a truly random sample. Here is a listing of the schools, indicating something of the sociological structure of each:

1. Montufar. A military boys' public school located in the south end of Quito. Students come mostly from lower and middle class homes. 206 interviewed.

2. San Gabriel. A Catholic boys' school, catering mostly to a higher class clientele. 134 interviewed, all juniors.

3. Benalcazar. A public, nonsectarian boys' school drawing mostly from the middle and upper classes. It is considered to be unusually excellent academically. 85 interviewed.

4. Colegio de America. This is a girls' school known for its discipline, catering mostly to the rising middle class. 195 interviewed.

5. Anderson. This school was begun by the Mission Covenant Church and now is almost entirely Ecuadorian in administration. It still is a private school, with many Christian families sending their children there. 84 interviewed.

6. Americana. This is a private coeducational school, bilingual in presentation, catering to the upper economic and social classes. 106 interviewed.

Questionnaires were administered in classroom settings. The sponsorship of the survey never was made known, and there was no bias from that source. Frequently a school official in charge of Secondary Orientation administered the questionnaire. Quito students, by the way, have received many surveys and were used to this type of anonymous interrogation.

A total of 810 usable questionnaires resulted. Cooperation from the schools was unusually good. In fact, all asked to receive copies of the results. Interviewing was completed by the first week in June.

Editing, Coding, and Tabulation

Starting on June 3, all of the cooperating graduate students in the program were called into a central location to initiate the laborious process of editing and coding. There were some additional volunteers from the HCJB staff. Coding was necessary because of the large number of open-end questions. Large eighty-column sheets were utilized for this purpose, and the coding task consisted simply of recording the appropriate number to be punched in each column. This proved to be time-consuming, and the task was finished on June 9.

On June 10 a mission official on a trip to the United States delivered the questionnaires to Wheaton. The questionnaires then were keypunched and tabulated, using the Wheaton College facilities. The computer output consisted of straight tabulations and percentages as well as cross tabulation of all questions by age, sex, school, ownership of television in the home, ownership of a telephone in the home, attendance at religious services, religious preference, and the person with whom the respondent lived. Statistical significance of the differences was assessed through use of chi square analysis. Tabulation was finished and computer data was delivered to Quito on July 1.

A "Thank You" Contact

Special letters were sent to the General Director of Education and to the principals of cooperating schools on June 24. This step of appreciation always is significant, especially when expatriots are conducting research in a country other than their own.

Data Analysis and Interpretation

As part of a course in Communication Strategy, two teams each consisting of eight missionaries undertook the task of data analysis and formulation of strategy. This was initiated on July 1 and completed by the end of August, at which time an oral report was given to leaders from missions and church groups in Quito. The final written report was presented to the field Council of HCJB during September. It was accepted in principle and approval given for initial implementation.

THE FINDINGS

Space does not permit a complete discussion, and the reader is referred to the detailed findings in Figure 26. This section is confined to highlights.

Spiritual Practices and Beliefs

The data presented in Figure 27 indicate that the majority of the students claimed a Roman Catholic background. Yet, cross tabulation by age showed that their interest in religion and acceptance of its beliefs declined sharply with maturity. Most are not agnostic, but there was definite confusion on the basic facts about Jesus Christ and His teaching. The majority would be at about stage -6 on the model of spiritual status presented earlier.

It is encouraging to note that approximately 60 percent indicated interest in knowing about other religions. Thus, the modification in religious beliefs and practice does not necessarily reflect a decline in interest in spiritual matters.

Figure 28 documents some of the needs these students expressed. The significant areas were security, stability, acceptance, and belonging. These young people were trying to cope with the capricious educational system. They worried about political instability, loneliness, finding a job, family problems, and marriage. There were some differences between boys and girls in these responses. As might be expected, the girls were more interested in marriage and romance, but most needs were common to both.

ORTHODOX - BELIEFS

PROFESSED RELIGION:

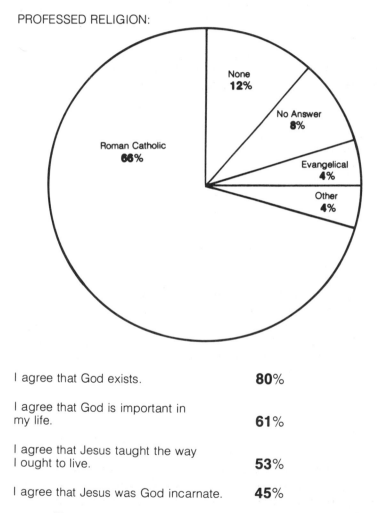

I agree that God exists.	**80**%
I agree that God is important in my life.	**61**%
I agree that Jesus taught the way I ought to live.	**53**%
I agree that Jesus was God incarnate.	**45**%

Figure 27. Religious Backgrounds of Quito Students

How Can I Get Them to Listen?

NEEDS:

	AGREE
I want to know more about birth control.	79%
I want to know more about other religions.	56%
At times I feel lonely.	48%

CONCERNS:

	CONCERNED
I am afraid of failing this school year.	79%
I am afraid of a political crisis in Ecuador.	73%
I'm concerned about finding the right person to marry.	60%
I don't know what work I'll do in the future.	68%
I'm afraid I won't find a work which I'll like.	64%
I don't get along with my parents.	54%
I'm concerned about my family situation.	65%

Figure 28. Dominant Needs and Concerns of the Quito High School Student

Media Exposure

How can these youth be reached? The data in Figure 29 reveal that radio is listened to more than television, although the margin of difference is small. The favorite time of day is afternoon and evening. The top three radio stations all feature both North American and Latin rock music. The favorite music was

162

foreign rock, followed by Latin rock, foreign popular music, and
Latin popular music.

Television Ownership	**95%**

Watch TV more than 1 hour daily — **40%**

Listen to radio more than 1 hour daily — **51%**

Over two-thirds prefer afternoon or
evening for radio listening

FAVORITE RADIO STATIONS:

1º   Radio Vision — **33%**

2º   Radio Musical — **23%**

3º   Radio Melodia — **16%**

4º   Radio Presidente — **11%**

5º   Radio Central — **3%**

6º   HCJB (AM & FM) — **3%**

INDICATED MUSIC PREFERENCE:

1º   Foreign Rock

2º   Latin-American Rock

3º   Foreign Popular

4º   Latin-American Popular

Figure 29. Mass Media Exposure of Quito High School Students

Demographic Characteristics

The sample was composed of 67 percent boys and 33 percent girls ranging in age from 16 to 20. Most still lived at home with their families. The high incidence of television and telephone ownership was an indication of at least middle-class status. It was interesting to compare the students' professional aspirations with the status of parents. The most frequent parental profession was businessman, followed by blue-collar worker, with engineering rating a poor third. The students, however, were striving first for an engineering career, followed by medicine and architecture. Thus, they were moving up the social scale, a process which tended to make them open to a new life style.

THE COMMUNICATION STRATEGY

A twelve-month strategy was designed to reach these youth both through the mass media and through personal evangelism.

Goals

Several conclusions were reached in the goal-setting process. First, every effort was made to avoid an evangelistic outreach which would die without truly affecting the local church. Next, it became apparent that determined efforts were required to achieve cooperation of the churches. Finally, churches had to be helped both in reaching and discipling young people if there were to be lasting effects.

It was realized that a doubling of all church youth groups still would result in reaching less than one percent of all Quito youth. Personal evangelism thus could not be the only activity at this point. The only way to reach most of the 68,000 in the target audience was through the mass media.

Church Growth Goals. The church was the heart of the strategy, and the following specific goals were set:
1. A 50 percent increase in the size of all participating youth groups.

2. A total of ten churches would be involved in the outreach.
3. A vital youth group would be established in each participating church.
4. The following responses would be achieved among youth in these youth groups:
   a. 35 percent would share their faith in the next month.
   b. 55 percent would invite a friend to the group in the next month.
   c. 40 percent would say that they were being fed spiritually in their church, including the youth group itself.

These were the goals only for the first year. By the end of the second year, it was anticipated that more churches would participate and that all responses would be increased.

Communication Goals. The following evangelistic goals were set:

1. Spiritual awareness:
   a. An increase from 61 percent to 71 percent in those who said that God was important to them.
   b. An increase from 53 percent to 68 percent in those who said that Jesus taught the way to life.
   c. An increase from 45 percent to 56 percent in those who said that Jesus was God incarnate.

2. Spiritual answers to felt need:
   a. 60 percent who agreed that Jesus offers help in coping with loneliness.
   b. 60 percent who agreed that Jesus offers help in coping with the future.
   c. 60 percent who agreed that Jesus offers solutions to family problems.
   d. 60 percent who agreed that Jesus offers help in making friends.

3. Program awareness:
   a. 70 percent who could recognize the radio and newspaper theme, "Algo Nuevo" (something new).
   b. 30 percent who could remember some of the content of a recent radio show or newspaper.

165

Contrary to the usual evangelistic campaign, there were no goals with respect to numbers of decisions. This reflects the concept of evangelism and spiritual decision processes outlined in the companion volume by the author and H. Wilbert Norton.[1] Awareness of basic spiritual facts must be established before personal evangelism can have much payoff. Moreover, people do not listen if there is no focus on felt needs. Therefore, these goals have the intent of moving people in their decision processes to the point of receptivity to a personal presentation of the plan of salvation. The major focus, in turn, is to help the local church build an attractive youth program and a dynamic group of believers who, at a later point, can be effective in "reaping" the harvest.

The Strategy

The proposed strategy has two distinct components: (1) training of church leaders; and (2) outreach through the mass media and personal evangelism.

The Training of Leaders. A four-phase program was developed which commenced with helping pastors and leaders become aware of the needs of young people. Later stages led to a training program and the initiation of new youth programs in the cooperating churches. A series of materials and training aids was proposed for this purpose.

Evangelistic Outreach. The mass media thrust centered on a radio show to be run on a commercial station and an "underground" newspaper to be distributed on campus. Both were to be entitled "Algo Nuevo" and would focus on the needs of the youth and building a progressive awareness that Jesus Christ provides the answers. Along with these media, a telephone hotline would be used for on-the-spot counseling.

The Algo Nuevo theme seemed to be an effective "integrator." Many students gave evidence of feeling trapped by

---

[1]Engel and Norton, *What's Gone Wrong?*

circumstances. The theme thus spoke to their dilemma and served to attract attention.

It was intended to use one of the top three radio stations and to run the program in a two-hour block if possible. The program would be "up-tempo" in music and format. A sample program was taped and pretested on youth with excellent results.

The Algo Nuevo newspaper would be distributed free at all high schools. It was to be a single-folded sheet with high visual impact again speaking forcefully to the needs and concerns of the audience.

The telephone hotline was a way to involve the youth presently involved in cooperating local churches. They were trained for telephone counseling, and they were encouraged to make personal contact with those who called in.

There were some additional components of this campaign also, including newspaper advertisements, bus posters, and other forms of promotion of the radio program. The calendar of events is in Figure 30. There would be an evaluation and review both at the midpoint and at the conclusion. The budget for one year was $16,400.

COMMENTARY

This chapter has reviewed a research project in Quito, Ecuador. Notice that all phases were adapted to the Ecuadorian situation. Researchers won governmental cooperation at the outset. The questions were developed and pretested in cooperation with national leaders, and the wording proved to be appropriate for the circumstances. Students responded with interest. Moreover, they used a range of categories of agreement and disagreement, providing at least a partial indication that they were revealing true feelings and were not just indicating what they were "supposed to say." The guarantee of anonymity was absolutely essential for this purpose.

There was no real way to draw a random sample given the

How Can I Get Them to Listen?

(Months from the beginning)

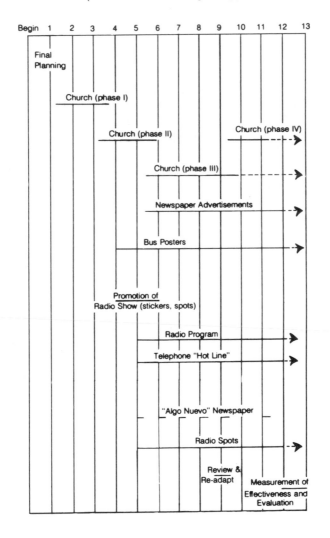

Figure 30. Calendar of Events for Algo Nuevo

realities of the situation. Yet the sample was representative. In this instance, good managerial projection could be made to the total population, even though this was not possible statistically.

The resulting strategy flowed logically from the data itself. All program components were pretested using the methods discussed in chapter 6.

No one can say at this point what the final outcome of this program will be. Without this environmental analysis, however, there would have been no factual basis for such a strategy.

10

Phasing Research Into Strategy

Now the final report has been made, but there is one remaining question: "Will the findings ever influence organizational strategy?" This issue is far from academic, because organizations, both secular and Christian, have tendencies to embrace managerial practices which virtually guarantee that the report will do little more than grace a library shelf.[1] It is the purpose of this chapter to examine some of these managerial obstacles and to advance some suggestions for solution.

Some Obstacles to Research-Based Strategy

The Accountability Barrier

"It wasn't my fault" is a phrase found in the vocabulary of all peoples. This pervasive reluctance to being held accountable is always more covert than overt in the Christian organization, but it is there nonetheless. Consider the following scenario.

Fred Leonard has recently joined the staff of the Christian radio station in Rollingwood — WTLT (Winning the Lost Today). Some readers will recognize Fred as a key figure in *What's*

---

[1]For a fascinating discussion of how these foibles can creep into the Christian organization, see James L. Johnson, *The Nine-to-Five Complex* (Grand Rapids, Mich.: Zondervan Publishing House, 1972).

Gone Wrong With the Harvest? Fred has recently joined WTLT from a secular station where he held a similar position as program manager.

One of Fred's first actions was to subscribe to a secular program rating service which documents the actual listening audience of stations in a given market. These figures showed that WTLT had a total listening audience per quarter hour of 0.25 percent of all who were listening to radio at that time. Fred was not surprised, and he suspected that most of these were already Christians.

A report was presented to the Board of Directors, and here was their response: "You have to realize, Fred, that Christian work is different from the secular world from which you came. We have prayed over our station format, and we believe that God would have us leave it just as it is. Couldn't you imagine what our church friends would say if we became more worldly in our sound?"

This example, of course, is apocryphal, and no offense is intended whatsoever. But it does illustrate a common response to research — *spiritualizing away the problem.* What could Fred now say? He too had prayed over this problem, and it became unmistakably clear that the station was failing in its expressed purpose of evangelistic outreach. The spiritualized response completely closed the door to further discussion.

Jesus never allowed the luxury of spiritualization. The doctrine of stewardship reiterated in so many ways in both the Gospels and in the Epistles speaks to the fact that God has given His church a role to perform. The avoidance of accountability is nothing more than avoidance of stewardship. This, in the final analysis, is a spiritual issue and not a managerial one. Need we say more?

An Improper Concept of Management

We stressed in an earlier chapter that most principles of modern management really have their roots in the Proverbs. This is an important point to grasp, because it underscores the value offered by contemporary management literature.

Here are just a few of the improper concepts of management which can affect both the acceptance and the use of research. The first is what the author has come to label the "big man syndrome." One well-known Christian leader is famous for his doctrine that "Any Christian organization is the lengthening shadow of a great man." While strong leadership is always a necessity, this kind of thinking usually leads to an organization centered around one individual. Often they serve as intolerable bottlenecks to any kind of action. But, even more seriously, leadership is not developed at the lower echelons where the real action is implemented.

Dominant leaders of this type often are quite intuitive in their approach. I have made it clear that I respect this intuition, but it is distinctly limited in a world of future shock. Such a person often is suspicious of research. He either will not permit it to be undertaken or will inhibit its implementation if any kind of major change is required.

The essence of modern management is development of people to perform their functions efficiently and effectively. This never will happen if lower echelon managers are not given the required tools, one of which is research. The dominant man approach fails to set the climate at the top which is so essential if an organization is to adapt to a changing environment.

The Square Peg in the Round Hole

In theory, people are promoted because of demonstrated ability to perform. In reality, there are many other reasons for promotion which have nothing to do with ability. The net effect is that people can be assigned to jobs in which they cannot perform as intended for reasons of ability, temperament, or spiritual maturity.

I have encountered examples where research has been shelved for the reason that it proved to be a threat to the manager who, in reality, was a square peg pounded into a round hole. One example was mentioned in chapter 2. No criticism is intended of such individuals, because misplacement usually is not their fault. The circumstances they face can lead to a deep-seated sense of inferiority which simply will not allow them to face the facts squarely in any situation.

The Christian organization has no excuse for misplacement. First, and of greatest importance, God has equipped His church with gifts to carry out its work under the headship of Christ. Job assignments in both the church and parachurch organization must take spiritual gifts into account. Unfortunately this tends to be forgotten. Second, our Lord left the example that disciples must be *trained.* Until recently Christians have to a large degree been content with a grounding in the Bible and theology. These, of course, are foundational, but God never intended His Word to be a management textbook. Christians have erroneously looked askance upon the behavioral sciences and management theory. It is small wonder that many leaders are unequipped to perform their function. Fortunately this outmoded thinking is rapidly giving way to serious management training.

The Tyranny of the Urgent

Most of us, myself including, have another common phrase in our vocabulary: "If I only had the time." The realities of our lives force us to center attention on the urgent, and much that is important gets laid aside for this reason.

It is well to consider a quote which has been attributed to the late Dwight D. Eisenhower: "The urgent is seldom important and the important is seldom urgent." This is a call for continual evaluation of priorities. What is *really* important?

An organization which centers on the important rather than upon the urgent usually is characterized by a sense of ongoing adaptation to the changing environment. All types of information are sought and utilized. Research thrives in such a setting and provides the very "eyes and ears" which management must have to keep abreast of circumstances. On the other hand, there is little role for research if energy is devoted mostly to "firefighting" and coping only with the urgent.

Undue Deference to Clientele

Most churches and parachurch organizations are dependent upon voluntary contributions for their life. This, of course, demands a sensitivity to this clientele and a willingness to listen to their suggestions. The problem enters when clientele are allowed to develop a stranglehold on organizational strategy.

One missionary radio organization analyzed its listening audience and determined that major programing changes were required. Unfortunately, this station can be picked up by radio receivers in the United States. Within a short time mission headquarters was bombarded with complaints about these changes. Shortly thereafter, all change was reversed and programing restored to its former content. The outcome, of course, was a waste of thousands of dollars of research, to say nothing of the devastating effect on staff morale. Other examples could be given as well.

Why are clientele so frequently allowed to gain the upper hand? The primary reason is failure to educate them in the purposes of the strategy. Everyone responds with the light he has. Once reasons are explained, particularly in the context of biblical principles, most people are reasonable.

There may be times when education is undertaken and key donors still threaten to withhold support. It is at this point where management must face the question of who sets the agenda, the sheep or the Shepherd? Financial realities obviously must be faced, but undue deference to the clientele can result in a quenching of the Spirit. It must never be forgotten that God has promised to provide full resources for those who are doing *His work.*

DEVELOPMENT OF A RESEARCH-BASED PERSPECTIVE

A commitment to research implies change, and change will not take place in an environment which is antithetical to it. Yet, it is possible to build a proper perspective, especially if attention is given to some essential attitudes and working practices.

Delegation of Both Authority and Responsibility

The job description is the working document for anyone functioning in a complex organization. It spells out the details of the person's tasks and specifies the limits of both authority and responsibility. The most common shortcoming is for higher management to delegate authority for a task without the corresponding responsibility for implementation. If lines of responsibility are hazy and indefinite, research recommendations never will be implemented, even though they are endorsed from the top. This obvious and fundamental point represents the greatest single deterrent to research the author has encountered in nearly twenty years of service as a consultant to all kinds of organizations, both secular and Christian.

Development of Proper Research Motivation

It was heavily stressed at the outset that research must be undertaken for the right reasons. It is especially essential that those who are responsible for implementation must have a thoroughgoing commitment to change if research is to be anything other than counterproductive.

Much of the responsibility here lies with the researcher. It is his or her role to assess the limits of change that decision makers can and will accept and then function within those limits at any point in time. More technically, they must act in the role of a *change agent.* [2] A change agent always assumes the perspective of the decision maker without losing sight of the ultimate objective. The key here is patience — a willingness to let change take place over time at a pace which will be accepted by those in the organization. This attitude can be difficult to learn, but it is essential if a research perspective ever is to develop.

---

[2]See Lyle E. Schaller, *The Change Agent* (Nashville: Abingdon Press, 1972).

Phasing Research Into Strategy

A Reliance on the Leadership of the Holy Spirit

At several points the author has stressed that the source of barriers to change is more often spiritual than managerial. In other words, man can, by his actions, short-circuit the leadership of the Spirit. We are told in Proverbs 16:9 that we should make plans, but remember that *the final outcome is always in God's hands.* Once it is grasped that man and God work together in this process, then the decision maker has little choice but to be accountable and open to change. Personal fears and motivations fade in importance when God is placed in His proper place as Lord of life.

A FINAL WORD

So here we have it — a review in nontechnical terms of the steps in research design and implementation. Now, what should the reader do from this point on?

The first thing is obvious — get started! The greatest difficulty always lies in definition of research objectives and commitment to change. Research design itself is mostly a matter of technique which is learned through experience. Thus, the beginning step is to ask the right questions. Then begin to undertake some noncomplex projects to get at the answers. Methodological mistakes probably will be made, but it is more costly to maintain the status quo.

There is a great need to develop research expertise within the Christian organization — both church and parachurch. Even though most readers can carry out projects of the type discussed in this handbook, many aspects of research design could not be covered here because of their complexity. In short, there is more to research technology than this manual can convey. There is a definite need for trained researchers. Some help can be gotten from the books cited throughout, but there is no doubt that one learns the more complex aspects of research by carrying out projects under qualified supervision. Universities throughout the world offer courses in either marketing research or communications research. Take advantage of such resources. Also do not be hesitant to call upon qualified consultants for help.

Finally, never forget that research does not replace intuition and experience. It merely augments them and helps to reduce error in decisions. Moreover, it is never a substitute for the guidance of the Holy Spirit. Rather, it is a means of providing the fact which the Spirit uses as He leads. Always remember that the objective is development of a research-based, Spirit-led strategy.

For Further Reading

Ansoff, H. Igor (ed.). *Business Strategy.* Baltimore, Md.: Penguin Books, Inc., 1969. (A basic source on planning)

Bross, Irwin D. J. *Design for Decision.* New York: The Free Press, 1965. (Classic source on decision making and modern tools)

Dayton, Edward R. *Tools for Time Management.* Grand Rapids, Mich.: Zondervan Publishing House, 1974. (Christian perspective on management)

Drucker, Peter F. *The Effective Executive.* New York: Harper & Row Publishers, 1967. (An indispensible source for executive effectiveness)

Ferber, Robert (ed.). *Handbook of Marketing Research.* New York: McGraw-Hill Book Company, 1974. Part I (Introduction to research process in a complex organization).

Gangel, Kenneth O. *Competent to Lead.* Chicago: Moody Press, 1974. (A Christian perspective on leadership)

Goodenough, Ward H. *Cooperation in Change.* New York: Russell Sage Foundation, 1963. (Highly anthropological source on the change agent process, of special value for missionaries)

Schaller, Lyle E. *The Change Agent.* Nashville, Tenn.: Abingdon Press, 1972. (Excellent, readable introduction to the Christian and the change agent process)

Wiwcharuck, Peter G. *Christian Leadership Development and Church Growth.* Revised edition. Manila: Christian Literature Crusade, 1973. (Helpful source on management of the Christian organization)

Glossary

AIO QUESTIONS: Analysis of life style through questions on activities, interests, and opinions.

AMBIGUITY: A bias in questionnaire design in which the meaning of the words used is not clear to the respondent.

AREA CLUSTER SAMPLING: A sampling method which focuses on selection of only certain geographic areas or clusters within the larger area.

BIAS: Errors and mistakes in the process of research design which cause the findings to deviate from the literal truth.

CHI SQUARE ANALYSIS: A statistical procedure to test whether differences between two or more percentages are due to chance variations.

CLASSIFICATION INFORMATION: Descriptive information about people such as age and income.

CODING: The assignment of numbers to questionnaire responses to permit entry onto a computer tabulating card.

CONFIDENCE INTERVAL: The area of estimated values of the sample within which the true value falls with a predetermined probability (usually 95 percent).

CONVENIENCE SAMPLE: Selection of people primarily on the basis of speed and low cost with every effort made to achieve a representative sample.

COST/BENEFIT ANALYSIS: The comparison of costs of a particular research design with the benefits to be achieved.

CROSS TABULATION: The sorting of data into subgroups within the overall sample to determine if there are response variations on important questions.

DEMOGRAPHIC INFORMATION: Another way to describe classification information such as age, income, social class, and education.

DESCRIPTIVE SURVEY: A "snapshot" of reality at any given point in time achieved through use of questionnaire methods.

ERROR: A statistical term describing the extent to which data collected through sampling fails to reflect the true data in the population or universe.

EDITING: Evaluation of completed questionnaires to ascertain whether they have been filled out according to instructions.

EXPERIMENT: A method of research design in which all things are held constant while one or more factors are varied systematically to reveal the effects of these variations.

INCENTIVE: Some form of inducement to encourage response to a direct mail questionnaire.

INDECKS SYSTEM: A manual punchcard system allowing data tabulation without the use of a computer.

INTERVIEWER BIAS: Systematic errors introduced into the data collection process knowingly or unknowingly by the interviewer.

LOADING: Question wording biased in such a way that one response is favored over another.

MANAGERIAL SIGNIFICANCE: A difference between responses given by members of various sample subgroups sufficient to warrant managerial action. Usually defined to be a difference of 10 percent or more.

NONPROBABILITY SAMPLING: Samples chosen without explicit consideration given to randomness.

MISPERCEPTION: Questionnaire bias in which the words used lie outside the experience of the respondent.

OBSERVATION: A method of research in which data is collected by nonobtrusive methods without the use of a questionnaire and direct interaction.

OPEN-END QUESTIONS: A question format in which the response categories are not specified, often followed by probing for further detail.

POPULATION: The target group from which a sample is selected.

PRETESTING (QUESTIONNAIRE): Trial use of a questionnaire on small numbers of people to verify that questions communicate as intended and are correctly understood.

PRETESTING (STRATEGY): Research undertaken prior to the actual execution of a communication strategy to verify that all the details of the strategy are correctly designed for the target audience to accomplish stated goals.

PROBABILITY SAMPLES: Samples designed in such a way that each respondent has a known and equal chance of being selected.

PROBES: Additional questions used following nonstructured questions to clarify responses and inquire more deeply.

PSYCHOGRAPHIC RESEARCH: Another term for analysis of life style through questions on activities, interests, and opinions (AIO questions).

PURPOSIVE SAMPLE: A nonrandom sampling method in which individuals or groups are chosen through the judgment of the researcher as being representative of the population.

QUOTA SAMPLE: A nonrandom sampling procedure in which respondents are selected by the interviewer in proportion to various characteristics within the population — i.e., age, sex, etc.

RANDOM SAMPLE: (See Probability samples).

RESEARCH: The collection of information useful in planning.

RESEARCH DESIGN: The overall methodology followed in structuring the research inquiry.

REPRESENTATIVENESS: The basic sampling criterion specifying that the final sample mirrors the target population in all significant details.

RESPONDENT: The person chosen to be interviewed.

SAMPLE: A subgroup of a larger population chosen for purposes of a survey.

SELECTIVE ATTENTION: Audience avoidance of unwanted communication messages.

SELECTIVE DISTORTION: Audience miscomprehension of unwanted communication messages.

SELECTIVE RETENTION: Audience forgetting of unwanted communication messages.

SEGMENTATION: Isolation of homogeneous subgroups within a total audience who show signs of communication receptivity and their consequent designation as target audiences.

SIMPLE RANDOM SAMPLE: A sample chosen by random means from a homogeneous list of respondents.

STATISTICAL SIGNIFICANCE: Designation of a difference between two or more responses given by subgroups within the sample as *not* being due to chance. They are, in other words, real differences (or at least differences unlikely to have occurred by chance, given the confidence level chosen).

STRAIGHT TABULATION: Numerical counting of frequencies and computation of percentages.

STRATA: Subgroups within a population or sample.

STRATIFIED RANDOM SAMPLING: A sample chosen from a heterogeneous population list so that the sample reflects the varying strata within the population.

Glossary

STRUCTURED, DISGUISED QUESTIONS: Question design in which the intent of the question is made nonevident and response categories are specified.

STRUCTURED, UNDISGUISED QUESTIONS: Question design in which the intent of the question is made evident and response categories are specified.

SYSTEMATIC SAMPLING: Division of a population list into intervals and then choosing names from within those intervals.

SURVEY: Use of the questionnaire method.

TABLE OF RANDOM NUMBERS: A list of numbers with no internal ordering used in selection of a sample.

TABULATION: Numerical counting of the responses.

TRADEOFF: A balancing of costs and benefits to arrive at a decision in the research design process.

UNIVERSE: (See Population).

UNSTRUCTURED, DISGUISED QUESTIONS: Question design in which the intent of the question is obscured and response categories are not specified.

UNSTRUCTURED, UNDISGUISED QUESTIONS: Question design in which the intent of the question is obscured and response categories are specified.

UNRESTRICTED RANDOM SAMPLE: (See Simple random sample).

VALIDITY: The extent to which the questioning process actually reveals the truth.

YEA-SAYER, NAY-SAYER BIAS: A tendency for some people to give a positive answer regardless of their true feelings.